THE LAST
Cowboys

THE LAST
Cowboys

Closing the Open Range
in Southeastern New Mexico,
1890s–1920s

Connie Brooks

Published in cooperation with the
Historical Society of New Mexico

University of New Mexico Press
Albuquerque

Library of Congress Cataloging–in–Publication Data

Brooks, Connie, 1941–
The last cowboys: closing the open range in southeastern
New Mexico, 1890s–1920s/Connie Brooks—1st ed.
p. cm. — (Historical Society of New Mexico
publications series)
Includes bibliographical references and index.
ISBN 08263–1423–6
ISBN 08263–1488–0
1. Cowboys—New Mexico—Lea County—History.
2. Cowboys—Llano Estacado—History.
3. Frontier and pioneer life—New Mexico—Lea County.
4. Frontier and pioneer life—Llano Estacado.
5. Ranch life—New Mexico—Lea County—History.
6. Ranch life—Llano Estacado—History.
7. Lea County (N.M.)—Social life and customs.
8. Llano Estacado—Social life and customs
I. Title.
II. Series.
F802.L4B47 1993
978.9'33—dc20 92–33399
CIP

Contents

Foreword

The Last Cowboys follows the lives of thirty-two cowboys of Lea County in southeastern New Mexico in the early part of this century. The lives of these men span the period from the post–Civil War long cattle drives from Texas, north to the railroads, to the end of the century and the closing of the era of open range cattle outfits in Texas and New Mexico. The author, Connie Brooks, identified some sixty cowboys and, of this group, she developed biographical information on thirty-two of them. Their lives are the subject of this book.

Brooks's scholarship is original, and the book makes a major contribution to the history of the American cowboy. This is a refreshing change from much popular western and cowboy writing. She has researched and written about the lives of these men without succumbing to myths that have accumulated as a result of Hollywood, dime novels, and television. Efforts in recent years by some writers to prove that the cowboy was not even of those myths but a social outcast of various persuasions are rebutted by Brooks. Her research deals with real people in real life. Brooks shows that the thirty-two cowboys of Lea County, New Mexico, after the closing of the open range cattle ranches, were productive citizens, bought houses, lived long lives, married, were literate, and contributed to the development of their various communities.

The Historical Society of New Mexico is proud to add this volume to the continuing series published in cooperation with the University of New Mexico Press. The current officers and members of the board of directors of the Society are: Robert R. White, President; John W. Grassham, First Vice President; Darlis A. Miller, Second Vice President; Andres J. Segura, Secretary; Spencer Wilson, Treasurer. Members of the board are: Susan Berry, Maurice M. Bloom, Jr., Thomas E. Chavez, John P. Conron, Richard N. Ellis, Elvis E. Fleming, Austin Hoover, Myra Ellen Jenkins, William J. Lock, Riley Parker, Agnesa Reeve, Albert H. Schroeder, Carl D. Sheppard, Robert J. Torrez, David Townsend, and John P. Wilson.

Spencer Wilson
Historical Society of New Mexico

Introduction

This book is about cowboys—cowboys who participated in one of the post-Civil War long cattle drives out of Texas or worked on one of the major open range ranching outfits prior to 1890 in Texas or New Mexico. Further, the cowboys about which this book is written eventually made their homes, at least for a time, in extreme southeastern New Mexico. Upwards of sixty such men have been identified, with considerable biographical data discovered about thirty-two of them. These thirty-two cowboys comprise the heart of this book.

Perhaps the greatest luxury an author has is one of definition: defining parameters, delimiting populations, and censoring data. The limitations of this study, however, were not entirely capricious. First, cowboys who participated in the long drives—who "went up the trail"—fall within the time period generally conceded by historians to have been the height of the cattle industry, 1866–1890. If a man participated in one of the long drives, he was deemed worthy of study. Second, if a man was employed by one of the sizable or historically noteworthy outfits, such as the XIT, the Spur, or the Matador in Texas, he is included in this book. Likewise, working for John Chisum or George Littlefield in New Mexico territory qualified a man for inclusion.

Third, cowboys were included if they became a statistic able to be enumerated; that is, if they settled in present-day Lea County, New Mexico, long enough to be examined. This third requisite for inclusion requires more explanation, as it is a less obvious parameter.

The Llano Estacado, or Staked Plains, of southeastern New Mexico was—and is today—a natural geographical extension of West Texas. In the 1880s, cattle herds were grazed across the line separating the State of Texas from the Territory of New Mexico as if no boundary line existed. It followed, then, that many of the men who worked as cowboys in Texas did the same in southeastern New Mexico. They were familiar with the country; so when it was time to settle down, they often chose the latter region for their homesteads. Because they left records of their lives, it was possible to include those particular cowboys in this book.

Moreover, open range ranching in southeastern New Mexico persisted well into the twentieth century, nearly twenty years after it has generally been conceded that the frontier had closed and open range ranching was at an end. Therefore, if the open range cowboys were not yet ready to settle down, they could still find a job working with cattle on a latter-day frontier in southeastern New Mexico.

What of these cowboys after the open range closed? Books (both scholarly and popular) about cowboys have dealt with particulars of the long drives or offered descriptions of day-to-day work performed by cowboys. Still other accounts have presented histories of open range outfits, biographies of notable cowmen, or tales told by sometimes overly enthusiastic cowboys. Yet little is known about individual cowboys. Demographic data have rarely been available. Few attempts have been made to discover what cowboys, as an occupational group, were like after their range work ended. Did they, as any factory worker might when his factory closed, find other employment? What became of them after their cowboy days were at an end?

This book, which originated as a master's thesis at the University of Oklahoma in 1989, was designed to discover more about the men who had, earlier in their lives, been the very boys that millions of Americans idolized. Were they mundane characters forever doomed to be stereotypical American heroes? Were they authentic heroes without whose help America's "destiny" would not have been manifested? Were they marginal characters who would never have found their niche had not open range ranching fortuitously occurred? These are some of the questions posed and answered in these pages.

The confines of the region and the presence of so many former open range cowboys in Lea County provided a natural laboratory. Perhaps it is true that generalizations about all cowboys should not be made from the thirty-two men whose lives are depicted here, but these findings are invaluable because they correct and revise inaccurate generalizations long ago placed in print.

Based upon my study of the thirty-two cowboys documented in Lea County, New Mexico, following the demise of the open range cattle industry, the following profile is characteristic: These men were literate, married, had children, owned permanent homes, lived long lives, and contributed to society as ranchers, farmers, and community builders in numerous other lines of work. The years they spent as cowboys appear neither to have marred nor glorified their lives. Not surprisingly then, this composite profile refutes many stereotypes about the American cowboy.

Acknowledgments

I am grateful to University of Oklahoma professors Jerome O. Steffen and William W. Savage, Jr., historians, and professor Richard L. Nostrand, geographer, for their illuminating remarks pertinent to this study, which began as a master's thesis under their direction. Their assistance, and especially Dr. Steffen's scholarly interest in me, has been invaluable. Any errors in this work, substantive or otherwise, are mine alone.

I am also grateful for good librarians everywhere, particularly those in my corner of the universe.

A special note of thanks goes to my husband Roy and daughters Natalie, Cheryl, and Leslie for their abiding faith in me.

1
The Place

At the same time as noted historian Frederick Jackson Turner was holding forth his frontier hypothesis, one of the last American frontiers was being penetrated on the Llano Estacado—the Staked Plains—of southeastern New Mexico. A part of the south plains of the Great Plains, this corner of the Territory of New Mexico was the last to be vacated by Indians, monopolized by open range ranchers, and furrowed by farmers. It was also the last place in New Mexico where buffalo grazed undisturbed, so it is not surprising that a few out-of-work buffalo hunters and Indian fighters first took up permanent residence on the Llano. Partly because of their successes in finding water and raising mustangs and a few rangy Mexican steers, cattlemen pushed onto the Llano to set up remote line camps and, later, headquarters for their open range operations. As elsewhere, permanent settlement was not far behind.

While some of the first ranchers to operate on a large scale in southeastern New Mexico were from the Pecos River region to the west and even from Arizona territory, most came from Texas where open range ranching had begun. Conditions making it favorable for these entrepreneurs of the Old West to eventually use the last corner of the great "Zahara" desert[1] have been documented elsewhere. Of importance here is the fact that in 1890, when the superintendent of the eleventh census was reporting that the frontier had been closed—that all the free western acreage had been settled[2]—one frontier still remained.

It was erroneously called a forbidden wasteland and an "anachronism . . . that persisted . . . well into the first quarter of the Twentieth Century."[3] The area that currently makes up Lea County consists of 4,390 square miles of high plains grama grass.[4] When the area was an unspoiled "last frontier," it included parts of both Chaves County and Eddy County, New Mexico territory. Statehood was achieved in 1912, and Lea County was formed in 1917. But because of its isolation, no predominantly Anglo town existed anywhere on the vast plains even in 1900. Two decades after the frontier had closed, the 1910 census in Eddy and Chaves counties revealed that the area that would become Lea County was populated by fewer than 1,500 families.[5]

Lea County, one of the last frontiers in the West, was settled with the help of numerous former open range cowboys from the Texas long drives and major cattle outfits. The area was settled late and sparsely, and even today the population density is only 14.8 people per square mile.[6] With an average annual precipitation of 15.47 inches[7] and an extremely conservative allocation of commercial water wells in New Mexico, ranching has always been the most efficient use of the land. The introduction of the windmill in the late 1880s made that fact overwhelmingly obvious. Had oil not been discovered beneath the semiarid soil in the early 1920s, in all likelihood the region would have remained one of tiny communities held together by a common interest in range grass and cattle.

When the first of the old open range cowboys came to the Llano Estacado, they found only bleaching bison bones and a few isolated water holes.[8] First came the great ranches, almost as the institution was eclipsing elsewhere.[9] Then came the small communities, with post offices established from 1900 to 1910, but the towns were miles apart and travel was difficult. There were no roads, save cattle trails, at first, and housing could hardly be termed anything but rough shacks and bleak dugouts.

In contrast, in the westernmost part of old Eddy and Chaves counties (west of present-day Lea County) were the towns of Carlsbad and Roswell, with daily trains, the Pecos River, telephones and telegraph, grand Victorian homes, and impressive public buildings. Even oysters on the half-shell, bedded in ice, were available to the west.[10] But in the eastern half of Eddy and Chaves counties—the portion that became Lea County in 1917—there was not even ice for drinking water. Water in Lea County was limited to a few surface lakes that did not last long in dry weather.

Lea was not alone in its great unpopulated expanses. In 1880, for example, in neighboring Gaines County, Texas, there were "only eight white men." Ten years later there were still only sixty-eight men living in Gaines County. By 1900 the population there had "slipped back to only five people," but by 1904 had grown to "better than 300."[11] In neighboring Terry County, Texas, in 1900, "only three ranchers were registered as owning land and actually making their home [there] . . . the others were itinerant cowboys whose real home was the saddle. . . ."[12] *(See Figure 1.)*

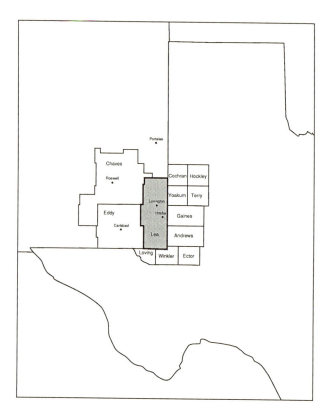

Figure 1. The Llano Estacado of Southeastern New Mexico and Environs.

By about 1890, present-day Lea County's northern half was the latter-day open range ranch known as the Four Lakes, or the LFD, after George Littlefield's brand. Littlefield had purchased part of John Chisum's holdings on the Pecos River at Bosque Grande[13] to the west of Lea County, and had moved into Lea in the late 1880s with the acquisition of the Four Lakes outfit.

South of the Four Lakes was the Hat Ranch with its headquarters at Monument Springs. Northeast of the Hat headquarters at the Texas line was a smaller open range outfit known first as the Mallett and later as the Highlonesome. *(See Figure 2.)*

South of the Hat Ranch were two major open range outfits—on the west, the San Simon (or Merchant Land and Cattle Company), which was established by Clabe Merchant, a major rancher who cofounded and named Abilene, Texas, and the JAL, operated by the Cowden brothers and stretching east from the San Simon to the Texas state line and beyond.[14] There were several smaller open range outfits among these four major ones and the Mallett/Highlonesome, and all these latter-day open range operations were possible places of employment for cowboys who had formerly plied that trade in their youth, had they wanted to work there.

The community of Monument, near Monument Springs on the Hat Ranch, was the first town in present-day Lea County, and several of the cowboys under investigation here lived in the neighborhood of Monu-

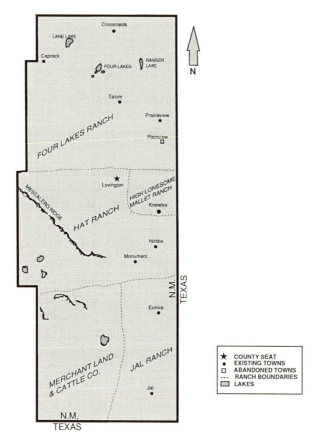

Figure 2. Open Range Ranches and Pioneer Towns, c. 1910 (adapted from Lea, New Mexico's Last Frontier, *with permission of the author, Gil Hinshaw).*

ment when they first settled in the region. Monument dates its existence from 1885, but its official post office was not begun until 1900. In 1904, the community of

Knowles began. In 1908 Lovington was begun, in 1909 Eunice and Tatum, and in 1910 Hobbs and Jal. Several smaller places functioned as tiny towns on the Lea County portion of the Llano before 1915, but they faded from existence for various reasons. Among them were the towns of Ranger Lake, Plainview, and Prairieview.

Most of the thirty-two cowboys in this study were rather ordinary, law-abiding citizens, but while the open range ranches were on the wane and the struggling little communities were trying to gain a foothold on the Staked Plains, the "enduring frontier was a haven for rustlers"[15] well into the early 1920s. And among the old open range cowboys studied was one cowboy rumored to be one of those rustlers.

Tom Ross is by far the most notorious of the cowboys who came to settle in Lea County, New Mexico. Ross appears to have begun working as a cowboy at about the age of thirteen, at which time he left home and never returned. As a young man, he reportedly was a member of the Red Buck Gang, which robbed and rustled along the Canadian River in Texas and in Indian Territory (Oklahoma). By the fall of 1889 he was working on the W. T. Waggoner Ranch in northcentral Texas. It has been suggested that Ross had a "low regard for foreign places and their people." Although undocumented, it has further been suggested that he killed a Chinese cook. Details are missing; but whether that incident is true, it is well documented that he did kill two men in Seminole, Texas, in 1923. Ross fled to Montana where he was surrounded by law enforcement officers in a bunkhouse and took his own life rather than be captured. He may have been partly "aimless drifter," as one author has written, but while he lived on the Llano Estacado he married, had a child, established a ranch, and joined a church.[16]

Herschel Robert "Gravy" Field, another cowboy, also lends some credence to the claim that the place had its share of outlaws. After leaving the XIT, Gravy went to Tucumcari, New Mexico, where he "shot a Mexican in a dispute during a gambling game." Gravy's friends helped him escape by rolling him in a bedroll, placing him over a horse, and camouflaging him in the remuda. He "rode on his belly out of New Mexico," so the story goes.[17]

Still another cowboy, Bob Beverly, claimed he spent time in his youth hanging out with outlaws on the Wichita ranges and in Indian Territory. He did not, however, claim to have broken any laws.[18] Three other cowboys from the thirty-two studied had stories involving fire-arms written about them, as will be seen later. Yet as colorful as these cowboys may have been, the other twenty-nine were upstanding citizens with traditional values. Indeed, even Ross, Field, and Beverly became good citizens of the county.

Being a cowboy and being a "gunslinger" were not mutually exclusive; neither were being a cowboy and participating in community building. All the thirty-two cowboys had the common experience of range work early in their lives; likewise, all participated in community building later in their lives. Tom Bingham began as a trail driver at the age of twelve; later he served two terms as Lea County tax assessor and served as the first probate judge in the county.[19] Jefferson D. Hart was vice president of the First Territorial Bank (1909–1920), vice-president of the Lovington School board for many years, and donated land for the Lovington cemetery.[20]

Allen Clinton "Daddy" Heard became one of Lea County's first commissioners when the new county formed, was vice-president of the First National Bank of Carlsbad, and served as a state representative (1920–1924).[21] Still others became the first postmasters, store owners, and played other roles critical to the establishment of communities.

Likewise, all of these cowboys took up homesteads, pre-emptions, or recently patented land. Contrary to popular myth, the cowboys who eventually settled in Lea County appeared eager to take up land and settle down. They became settlers of, if not the nester variety, at least the homesteader variety. And while a search for land unbroken by the plow is a common theme in cowboy mythology, it played a small role in the move west by these former cowboys.

Family tradition is perhaps patterned too often from the great overriding myths about cowboys. Today the families of the cowboys studied here frequently claim that their fathers and grandfathers were cowboys until they died. In truth, these cowboys homesteaded 160-acre parcels of arid land where gardening, a milk cow, or even a dryland farm operation were the norm. And they appear to have eagerly sought such homesteads.

As can be seen, then, the stage for these open range cowboys was a setting that can be said to have duplicated in many ways those earlier settings in Central and West Texas and elsewhere in the Trans-Mississippi West. The transformation of "place" was greatly aided by open range cowboys whose former work arena was, itself, transformed.

2
The Men

"He follows all sorts of logical trails until he can no longer ride down the road of life,"[1] claimed Cordelia Sloan Duke and Joe B. Frantz in their comprehensive study of XIT cowboys. As we shall see, in Lea County former open range cowboys clung to those logical trails, too; that is, when cowboying was no longer an option, preferred or otherwise, these former cowboys took up traditional occupations and led rather average lives.

Walter Prescott Webb observed that it was from the southern states that Texas drew its population,[2] and it has been well documented elsewhere that immigrants to Texas, at least during the mid-1800s, were somewhat stereotypical representatives of the Old South.[3] Others have claimed that the Southern influence in the cowboy tradition extended to a "reborn myth of the antebellum South," and a cowboy code that was a "Western and democratic version of the Southern gentleman's 'honor'."[4]

As for the thirty-two Lea County cowboys, "some were 'true gentlemen' of the Old South, intelligent and even cultured."[5] The South was an undeniable factor in their lives, for nearly all hailed from Texas, the Deep South, or peripheral states with southern traditions. Fifty-three percent were from Texas, primarily the north central region *(See Figure 3)*. Only three cowboys appear to have had little or no Southern influence in their upbringing.[6]

Bob Beverly was born in Ringold, Georgia, the son of a Confederate soldier who died of prolonged effects of the war, leaving Beverly orphaned at age twelve. Beverly was a literate man who spent his adult years writing magazine articles and books.[7]

Benjamin Franklin Davis, a South Carolinian, began his adult life by volunteering to serve with the Confederacy at age fourteen; he was a veteran of Shiloh and Muscle Shoals.[8] John Albert Lawrence was born in Alabama,[9] John Parish "Moster" Lewis was from Tennessee,[10] Tom Ross (who by all accounts was very gentlemanly, if an outlaw) hailed from Mississippi,[11] and Allie Rushing was Louisiana born.[12]

Stronger even than the Southern blood, at least mythologically, was the "cowboying" blood in these men's veins. In 1885, Joseph Nimmo, Jr., Chief of the U. S. Bureau of Statistics, proclaimed:

> During the last fifteen years the American cowboy has occupied a place sufficiently important to entitle him to a considerable share of public attention. His occupation is unique.[13]

Others, perhaps less inclined to elevate the status of the cowboy, have also viewed as unique the occupation of "cowboying."[14] Leaving aside a judgment on the accuracy of Nimmo's declaration, it seems important that one

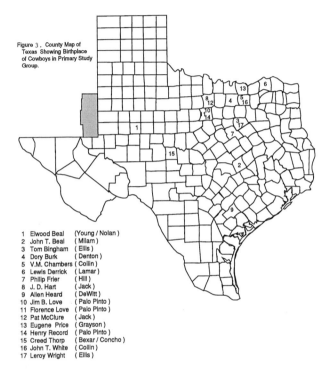

Figure 3 . County Map of Texas Showing Birthplace of Cowboys in Primary Study Group.

1	Elwood Beal	(Young / Nolan)
2	John T. Beal	(Milam)
3	Tom Bingham	(Ellis)
4	Dory Burk	(Denton)
5	V.M. Chambers	(Collin)
6	Lewis Derrick	(Lamar)
7	Philip Frier	(Hill)
8	J. D. Hart	(Jack)
9	Allen Heard	(DeWitt)
10	Jim B. Love	(Palo Pinto)
11	Florence Love	(Palo Pinto)
12	Pat McClure	(Jack)
13	Eugene Price	(Grayson)
14	Henry Record	(Palo Pinto)
15	Creed Thorp	(Bexar / Concho)
16	John T. White	(Collin)
17	Leroy Wright	(Ellis)

Figure 3. County Map of Texas Showing Birthplace of Cowboys in Primary Study Group.

examine how these cowboys perceived themselves. A consensus of former XIT cowboys was that they saw themselves simply as workingmen.[15]

Most of the cowboys in the primary study group *were* workingmen and *considered* themselves such. The families of some, though, resist the notion that their ancestors ever wanted to do anything but "cowboy," used in the vernacular as both noun and verb, as the following cases will illustrate. Philip Frier began "cowboying" (as his family called it) when he was twelve. As a young man he worked for the F Ranch near the Matador and later wrangled horses and broke broncs for the LFD. He came to Lea County in 1901, taking up a homestead. His family is fond of saying that he "couldn't get cowboying out of his blood," and that he aggressively worked on ranches, putting away every dime he could with the hope of someday owning his own spread. Yet Frier became a successful sheep rancher, the some-times-nemesis of a cowboy.[16]

Richard Heidel was thirteen years old when his father, who had immigrated from Germany, died. Heidel immediately struck out "cowboying," working north from Austin. About 1894 he worked for the XIT ranch helping survey for fences, scouting for expansion possibilities, and wrangling horses. It was on a scouting expedition that he first glimpsed the New Mexico side of the line, settling permanently in Lea County in 1910. Heidel's daughter claims "cowboying" was "all he knew to do," yet in later years he made his living as a farmer.[17]

Lea County cowboys easily—even hastily—got "cowboying" out of their blood by taking up other professions, too. Many, as had former XIT cowboys, went into law enforcement.[18]

Bob Beverly served as sheriff and tax collector for Midland County, Texas, from 1909 to 1912. From 1916 to 1921 he was cattle inspector for the Texas and South-western Cattle Raisers Association; 1923–1930, brand inspector for Lea County; 1933–1937, sheriff of Lea County.[19] Tom Bingham was deputy sheriff at Hobbs and later Tatum, New Mexico.[20] After his days in the saddle, Benjamin Franklin Davis served as a deputy sheriff in Paint Rock, Texas, as a cattle inspector, and, later, as sheriff.[21]

Robert Florence Love (Lovington's second postmaster) was elected the second sheriff of Lea County, serving from 1921 to 1924, after which he operated a meat market and cafe.[22] Politics, however, appears to have been his primary interest.[23] Another, William Fletcher Weir, was a Texas Ranger.[24]

Eight local cowboys established small cattle operations or stockfarms (often erroneously referred to as ranches), but many of these held concurrent outside employment in order to feed their families. Among the occupations held were butcher, railroad worker, oilfield worker, school teacher, carpenter, postmaster, writer, freighter, and day laborer; some even became thieves.[25]

It is important to note that Lea County cowboys who later amassed large local ranches of their own referred to themselves as cow*men,* not cow*boys.*

And if one can believe that citizens are truthful when speaking to census enumerators, the occupations reported locally disagree with Dobie's claim that "no genuine cowboy ever ranked himself in the laboring class."[26] From among the entire population of what constitutes modern-day Lea County, only thirty-four persons on the 1910 census reported their occupation as cowboy. (And none of those thirty-four were the thirty-two cowboys studied here.)[27]

Works by Siringo or "Teddy Blue" Abbott "tell us what [the cowboy] thought of himself and the work he did."[28] But they appear to differ greatly from what is known of the thirty-two cowboys here.

Most people on Lea County's latter-day frontier, including the thirty-two cowboys, were experiencing hard times and subsistence living, even when they had relatively more than their peers. It follows, in a subsistence-level community, that the occupation listed most frequently from among the countywide population was farmer.[29] Stereotypical cowboys in literature may have despised farmers, but the thirty-two cowboys appear to have lived happily among farmers. Some, as reported before, actually *became* farmers.[30]

Eight Lea County cowboys entered politics, albeit at levels ranging from school board members and county commissioners to state representatives. In 1924 Florence Love was elected state representative from what was then Eddy County, serving a two-year term. He was elected county tax assessor from 1930 to 1934, as well. It has been said that rather than a cowboy, he considered himself a politician.[31] No cowboy here, however, attained the level achieved by James F. Hinkle, who worked for the CA Bar outfit and eventually became governor of New Mexico.[32]

The XIT study cited one cowboy who later attended college and became a lawyer.[33] Similarly, this study discovered one cowboy, Leroy Wright, who attended college,[34] and another, V. M. Chambers, who no doubt received some secondary education since he later taught school.[35] Educational levels of the other thirty cowboys were limited mainly to elementary schooling, but all could read and write, a fact which would seem to dispel the myths about illiterate cowboys.[36] The cowboys represent a varied but literate group: Jim Love preferred to have his wife read the newspapers to him;[37] "Moster" Lewis was a literate man who remained proud all his life of the fact that he had taught his wife to read;[38] Henry Record's favorite book was *Pilgrim's Progress.*[39]

Scholars are wont to remind a fascinated public that cowboys were merely hired hands,[40] and that the terms *hands* or *cowhands* were more commonly used than *cowboy.*[41] This study, however, does not support completely those generalizations. The terms *hands* and *cowhands* were not used at all in the census records studied, possibly due to the late date (1910), and the term *hired man* was chosen by only four cowboys, all of whom worked for the Cowden brothers on the JAL Ranch, and all of whom listed that only as their *relationship* to the head of the household, not their occupation.[42]

Lifestyles and value systems are an integral part of at least the popular approach to cowboy history. Modern cowboys and their admirers are quick to perpetuate the clean, All-American image of the cowboy. But at least one cowboy has been quoted as saying that most cowboys were "burned out with bad whiskey and disease ... had a dose of clap or pox ... [and] a were a scrubby bunch."[43] One noted scholar contends that "cowpunching as an occupation attracted an unfortunate breed. ..."[44] But Baron von Richthofen in his "Cattle-Raising on the Plains of North America" claimed that "among cowboys" were to be found "the sons of the best families."[45] The truth is probably that most were not "a drunken, gambling lot," but the few have carried the many.[46]

While the question of why any of these cowboys (or any others for that matter) chose that occupation in the first place remains unanswered, a few possible reasons can be suggested, including these: the Pied Piper effect, as young boys saw other young men working to move the great herds up the trail; "squeezed out" of families with numerous mouths to feed, young men often had few alternative occupations from which to choose.[47]

Most of the thirty-two Lea County cowboys were sons of Texas farmers, which meant that their family status certainly falls somewhere between the unfortunate and the well-to-do.

Five men, though, had their moments at the lower end of society in their brushes with the law. Cited earlier are Bob Beverly who flirted with lawlessness as a youth, and Gravy Field whose passions no doubt ruled when he killed a man in a gambling dispute. There was John Parish "Moster" Lewis, who began working on ranches at an early age: the Cross C, the XIT, and the Matador were reportedly some of them. He was shot in the arm over a stock water dispute, after which he told his assailant, "You have killed the old Jew." (Both men fired, but Lewis's shot missed the other man, suggesting that not all cowboys were aces with six–guns.)[48] And there was Benjamin Franklin Davis who, in a scene right out of a Hollywood western, shot another man for insulting his sister. But since the man lived, Davis was not prosecuted.[49] One could easily argue that none of these four cowboys was an authentic outlaw.

The one genuine outlaw in Lea County was Tom Ross. According to the only scholarly account of his life, he was a villain equal to anyone depicted in a Beadle dime novel or ever invented by Hollywood. He killed two Texas Rangers (and was tried and convicted for that crime), after which he escaped and killed another man in a petty squabble. But even Ross had his supporters— local folks and kin whose memories of him are at odds with the darker accounts.[50]

Stereotypical cowboys drank early, long, and hard, and this would presumably have taken its toll. The Lea County cowboys commenced that trade at an average age of sixteen, the youngest being only eight and the eldest being thirty. Of the thirty-two men, fully half were sixteen or under when they embarked on their cowboy careers. The average life span among these same cowboys was seventy-five years and eight months and the median age was seventy-six, with the youngest dying at the age of forty-seven from pneumonia. Six lived to be nonagenarians; eight lived to be octogenarians; and eight lived into their seventies. Five were over the age of sixty when they died. And of the four remaining men (each of whom lived only to his fifties), one was struck by lightning, one committed suicide, and the other two died of unknown causes.

Liquor was a passion for some of these old open range cowboys, but the lifespans reported above suggest that it is unlikely that liquor shortened their lives. "Papa couldn't hold his liquor," Jim Love's daughter has written, and Jim's brother Florence has also been labeled a chronic imbiber by some family members.[51] "Moster" Lewis reportedly died an alcoholic.[52] Yet Florence Love lived to be seventy-three and Lewis lived to be seventy-five. As for being dissipated by disease, there is no evidence of it, and as for being dissipated by whiskey, the presumption is false. Overall, the cowboys studied here appear to have been a very healthy population, liquor and all.[53] *(See Figure 4.)*

Good works among the cowboys in the primary study group were discovered. "Moster" Lewis, who apparently delighted in driving out nesters, donated land for Texas Tech University at Lubbock.[54] One eccentric old cowboy, Henry Record, liked to feed his horse in the kitchen of his extremely modest wooden abode. Yet this same cowboy served on the board of Hardin-Simmons University and amassed a fortune, which he left to the Baptist Childrens' Home in Portales, New Mexico.[55]

Some Lea County cowboys wrote their recollections and memoirs.[56] Jerome O. Steffen, in his *Comparative Frontiers: A Proposal for Studying the American West,*[57] suggests what should have been logical fodder for such remembrances: "Distance, bad weather, Indian raids, disease, and dissident farmers were all western manifestations of . . . obstacles" to any successful cattle venture or drive. Distance and weather were indeed topics of the recollections. But did these remembrances or any other written or spoken record suggest that the old open range

	YEAR BORN	PLACE BORN	AGE BEGAN COWBOYING	AGE MARRIED	TIMES MARRIED	NUMBER CHILDREN	AGE TO LEA COUNTY	YEARS LONGEVITY
Anderson	1872	GA	18	24	1	4	34	58
Beal, E.	1860	TX	16	50	1	1	40	52
Beal, J. T.	1848	TX	12	52	1	3	43	68
Beverly	1872	GA	12	23	5	5	51	86
Bingham	1872	TX	12	34	1	6	34	72
Breckon	1854	NY	14	21	1	5	30	66
Burk	1870	TX	8	27	1	5	39	97
Chambers	1868	TX	21	44	1	2	52	89
Cooper	1874	KS	18	27	1	8	40	84
Davis	1843	SC	28	39	1	7	66	91
Derrick	1863	TX	16	30	1	4	49	91
Eidson	1874	MO	16	35	1	1	20	92
Field	1876	AR	15	33	1	3	27	66
Frier	1870	TX	12	37	1	4	31	68
Hart	1861	TX	23	50	1	3	27	87
Heard	1858	TX	15	29	1	2	29	86
Heidel	1881	Ger	13	25	1	4	29	73
Knight	1866	IT*	24	24	1	4	38	61
Lawrence	1846	AL	24	25	1	11	38	70
Lewis	1864	TN	18	25	1	4	30	75
Love, J. B.	1873	TX	17	25	2	7	34	72
Love, R. F.	1870	TX	17	26	2	4	30	73
McClure	1872	TX	17	25	1	8	37	85
Price	1868	TX	22	21	1	9	24	84
Record	1872	TX	18	26	1	0	25	90
Ross	1872	MS	13	32	1	1	32	57
Rushing	1876	LA	14	27	1	7	24	77
Thorp	1868	TX	14	28	1	11	34	76
Walter	1872	Ger	13	38	1	4	50	84
Weir	1844	MO	30	37	1	7	62	93
White	1868	TX	18	26	1	1	38	58
Wright	1876	TX	18	34	1	4	27	47

*Indian Territory

Figure 4. Statistical Data for Cowboys in Primary Study Group

cowboys of Lea County considered themselves heroes? Did these remembrances romanticize their lives? The lives of the cowboys in this study appear to have been romanticized only by their modern-day descendants and a handful of observers.

Bob Beverly has been described as

> [O]ne of the most colorful . . . characters who ever forked a bronc or roped a steer and has had a large and interesting part in the winning of the west and the creation of its glamorous history which has been immortalized in songs and stories of the cowboys of former days.[58]

Closer to reality is the response of one elderly local citizen who, when asked if people when he was a child (circa 1915) ever talked about the cowboy days, responded, "It weren't nothing worth talking about."[59] Yet today descendants of the thirty-two cowboys often talk about an idealized frontier, a mythological "Old West," and their heroic cowboy ancestors.

Finally, whatever the reasons these men decided to become cowboys, one thing seems certain: it was not, literally, in their blood. No cowboy studied here (or discovered elsewhere) was the *son* of a cowboy. And no cowboy studied here produced a son who later called himself a "cowboy," though some offspring ranched or, from time to time, performed day labor for area ranches.[60] Indeed, nine of the cowboys in this study together had twelve children known to have been ranchers (three women and nine men, excluding those female offspring who became ranch women through marriage). Cowmen, ranchers, women on ranches—these are familiar terms. But none called himself or herself cowboy or cowgirl.

Their Families and Folkways

If it is true that cowboys despised women and children and avoided civilization at any cost, then one might expect that not only would all the old cowboys be gone, they would not have left descendants, for they would never have been born. But such was not the case. The old open range cowboys who peopled the Llano Estacado may not have been typical, but they were certainly of one mind: they were intent upon marrying and having children. Further, they were intent upon establishing communities and institutions that replicated those they had known in their past. Therefore, it can be inferred that the open range cowboys who eventually settled in Lea County, New Mexico, were not the stereotypical loners and social misfits that literature has suggested; they no more subscribed to exclusivity or cliques than any other working class individual.

For example, nine of the cowboys studied signed the original register of the Open Range Cowboys Association. They were Bob Beverly, Tom Bingham, Millard Eidson, J. D. Hart, Richard Heidel, "Moster" Lewis, Florence Love, Jim Love, and Henry Record.[1] Jim Love was purportedly not a "joiner,"[2] yet he was also a charter member of Woodmen of the World. Love's brother Florence was active as a Democrat and a Mason. Charlie Walter was a Woodman as well. And Henry Record must not have been the stereotypical loner either, for he rode in several Lea County Fair parades.[3] Exclusivity surely was a term foreign to Allen C. Heard for he "liked to entertain . . . and entertain lavishly."[4] There was, then, "very little difference in the intellectual or social" behaviors of cowboys and "eastern farm hands," or any other similar occupational group.[5]

Like frontier settlements created elsewhere, and particularly similar to those in West Texas, the last frontier of the Staked Plains of Southeastern New Mexico developed along predictable lines. Until about 1880, the region now comprising Lea County was devoid of any permanent settlers. Earlier, it had been thought that the area did not have enough water to sustain agriculture. But buffalo hunters who had seen the region stayed on after the buffalo were gone; and their successes with shallow hand-dug wells—and subsequently, the windmill—led open range cattlemen, principally from Texas, to enter the region. Finally, with the establishment of ranching enterprises and their need for employees, goods, and services, the establishment of towns was not far behind.

Certain folkways and pastimes were, from the outset, a part of the culture of Lea County, as they were elsewhere.[6] By far the favorite entertainment in West Texas at or shortly after the turn of the century was a picnic. This was true in Lea County as well. The open range cowboys under study here played a significant role in the proliferation of traditions in the area.

Allen C. Heard had an annual picnic at his Highlonesome Ranch, and the town of Lovington began a tradition of annual picnics near what would later be the courthouse square. The first such town picnic in Lovington coincided with the opening of Jim B. Love's general store there. The list of other activities included membership in clubs, organizations, and fraternal orders; school entertainments, singings, literary societies, and dramatic clubs; and private parties, quiltings, and dances. Former open range cowboys took part in all these activities, often instituting them.

Florence Love, also called Fiddle Case, played for most of the dances in and around the town of Lovington.[7] Dory Burk, who had often been talked out of his night duty on the trail so that he could sing at the campfire for other cowboys' enjoyment, participated in local singings.[8] Despite Ray Allen Billington's suggestion that "amidst the lonely atmosphere of the . . . plains," certain civilizations were discarded,[9] in Lea County it is evident that civilized notions were embraced and provided a continuous thread of culture.[10] It has also been suggested that, on a more primitive frontier, "cultural pursuits were ignored."[11] In Lea County, a modern primitive frontier, this was not the case. John Turner Beal began working as a cowboy at the age of twelve. Beginning in 1866, Beal and a partner freighted and worked cattle, making three trips up the Chisholm Trail to Abilene, Kansas, and two trips to St. Louis, the latter with his own cattle. On one such return trip, Beal hauled back five grand pianos for his and other pioneer families in Lea County.[12] Millard Eidson, who was just a teenager when he began cow work, eventually formed a partnership with the noted John Scharbauer of Midland County, Texas, and became one of Lea County's most prominent and influential ranchers. In later years, his days were often filled with games of bridge and his evenings with dances. He and his wife, along with several other couples, formed a local dance club.[13]

Larry McMurtry has been quoted as saying that a cowboy's behavior and masculinity took "little account of women."[14] Davis, in his "Ten Gallon Hero," has contended that cowboys, in addition to not being family men, had no interest in "the homes they left behind."[15] In describing the *real* cowboy, Davis wrote

> He . . . has no interest in children and considers men who have lived among women as effete. Usually he left his own family at a tender age and rebelled against the restrictions of mothers and older sisters.[16]

Each of the thirty-two Lea County cowboys married; further, all but one had children. And though they lived very long lives, only three of the cowboys had more than one marriage. The average age at which these cowboys "settled down" in Lea County was thirty-six, and the average age at which these same cowboys married was thirty-two. They had, on the average, four and one-half children. In 43 percent of the cases, the cowboys married after coming to Lea County, which suggests many of them deferred marriage until their working days on the range were over. However, in sixteen instances (57 percent of the cases) these cowboys married before settling in Lea County. And in two cases, the cowboys married and continued working at that occupation.[17]

These former open range cowboys, however, were not the group that called themselves cowboys when the census enumerator made his rounds. The group of thirty-four individuals, who as late as the 1910 census still chose to call themselves cowboys, had only three married men among them, with a combined total of only eight children.[18] This latter-day group of predominantly young men appear to have been examples of life imitating art—the art of pulp fiction.

Among the cowboys under study here, some had wives and children living with them at the employing ranches. Eugene Price wrote that for several years the Quinn Ranch was home for him, his wife, and his eldest child, who was then quite small.[19] The emergence of ranching families hastened the establishment of towns on the Llano Estacado. As first one and then another cowboy brought women and children to the plains, almost immediately agents of culture appeared—school teachers were hired and churches were built. For example, the community of Knowles, prior to 1910, had three general stores, a dry goods store, a newspaper, a drug store, a lumber yard, three black-smiths, a hotel, a restaurant, a millinery, two feed yards, a U.S. land office, a furniture store, a barber shop, a hardware store, a telephone exchange, a photo gallery, tailor, school, and several churches.[20]

The Love brothers were instrumental in community building. Florence established the first hotel in Knowles. Jim provided the automobile that served as public transport for the community and carried the mail to that town.[21] In the community of Lovington, which would later become the county seat of Lea, the Love brothers were also the town's first and second postmasters and its first and second mercantile operators.[22]

With seven others, Eugene Price founded the First National Bank in Lovington, donated land for the first school there, and served on the town's school board.[23] His civic actions were typical of those of his cowboy peers, for it was their intent to establish cultural institutions whenever possible.

Furthermore, when the flow of culture and social institutions did not come about as quickly as Allen C. Heard wished (nor in so grand a manner), he moved his wife and children west to the town of Carlsbad, now county seat of Eddy County. There he found a more settled and genteel community and resettled them in a huge Victorian mansion.[24] In short, the open range cowboys who came to Lea County were quick to provide continuity in institutions and culture; even more, they demanded it.

The former cowboys appeared proud of their newfound status as town citizens. Beyond the fact that they never called themselves *cowboys* (even though their modern-day descendants would like to think that they always considered themselves so), they actually announced their new occupations to the census enumerators, fixing them forever in history. Florence Love listed his occupation (and place) as retail merchant at a drygoods and grocery. His brother Jim Love listed driver/auto, as his occupation. Allen C. Heard named himself proprietor/cattle ranch. He had achieved a status well above that of open range cowboy, and he was quick to point out the difference to the census enumerator.[25]

In addition to building tangible community institutions, the thirty-two open range cowboys from Lea County were part of another kind of community building—the establishment of a "community of memory"[26] by means of what one scholar has called "invented tradition."[27] This was accomplished through Open Range Cowboys Association meetings, started formally in Lea County in 1938,[28] but informally as early as 1933.[29] The Lea County institution was preceded by similar organizations such as the Stamford Cowboy Reunion, 1896;[30] the Old Trail Drivers Association, 1915,[31] and the XIT Reunion, 1936.[32]

Instead of gathering together to talk about their former occupation or romanticizing their collective past, however, the association appears to have been primarily a way to "renew old friendships."[33] During its fifty year history, the gathering has been mainly a social one, albeit theoretically limited in attendance to those who worked on the open range or descendants of those who did. In truth, the "meetings" are potluck dinners where anyone with ties to Lea County's pioneering past is welcome, whether their fathers or grandfathers were actual open range cowboys or not. To this writer's knowledge, the conversations at these get-togethers have never revolved around what it was like to work on the open range, nor do the oldtimers discuss what it might have been like for their ancestors to have participated in a cattle drive. Instead, the conversations are about the weather and politics, with an occasional "horse tale" thrown in for spice.

Whether it was the Kansas quarantines of the 1870s or other reasons that caused the cattle drives to become a "fading memory,"[34] it seems clear from the long span of intervening years (about 1890 to 1933) that the oldtimers did not form associations simply to commemorate their residence in the West, nor was reminiscence[35] the probable primary purpose for establishment of the Open Range Cowboys Association. Thirteen of the thirty-two Lea County cowboys participated in the long drives, yet little evidence exists that they ever talked much about those experiences. Had glorification of their occupation or romantic reminiscing been the primary purposes for the association, it seems obvious that the association would have been formed much earlier. Instead, a simple renewing of friendships with those who had worked in the same 'closed factory' was more likely the purpose.

The weight of evidence gathered about the participation in community building by the open range cowboys under study suggests that they were not "excessively clannish,"[36] nor even moderately so. Further, the often-stated taciturnity among the cattle fraternity appears to have been over-stated or, if present, more a product of their Southern upbringing than anything inherent in their occupation.[37]

As for religion, the theme of the irreverent cowboy runs deep.[38] But the *Texas Live Stock Journal* in 1888 saw the question of a cowboy's beliefs differently:

> The average cowboy does not bother himself about religion. The creeds and isms that worry civilization are a sealed book to the ranger, who is distinctively a fatalist. He believes that when the time comes for him to go over the range nothing can stand death off. . . .[39]

Atherton stated it this way: "proximity to nature and the hazards of their occupation" reminded cowboys of their mortality.[40] Still another writer has formulated the nature thesis in religion in what he terms the "cowboy ideal": cowboys have no need of formal religion once they find a pure and natural environment.[41]

Other scholars suggest that it was not so much a choice as it was that young cowboys "lacked time and inclination" for religion.[42] Church-going, it has been suggested, was often left to "nesters and homesteaders."[43] Based on this observation (since most of the cowboys under study here eventually took up homesteads themselves), one might presume that attending church would become important to the thirty-two cowboys in this study, at least later in their lives. But evidence collected suggests that this was rarely the case. A couple of the cowboys may have 'gotten religion' in advanced years, but most did not. One did, however, become a "student of the Bible" late in life. Charlie Walter would "sit for hours and read and study the

Bible," in his elder years, and he was also one of the few cowboys who actually joined a church.[44]

In some cases ranch owners "worked in . . . religion and influenced the personal conduct" of cowboys at, for example, the XIT.[45] And for the most part the cowboys under study here were the sons of Christian parents; therefore, tradition held the men to a core belief that may have been more theoretical than practical.

As one contemporary writer has noted, "religion is one of the most important of the many ways in which Americans 'get involved' in the life of their community and society."[46]

In early-day Lea County, *churches* (but not *religion*) became the "center of the social life of the community" as had been the case in West Texas towns.[47] In other words, the cowboys may frequently have been involved in activities that took place within church buildings, but religious services were infrequently attended.

Revivals, camp meetings, and other less religious activities that occurred at church buildings were an important adjunct to the culture in which the cowboys participated. But as important a part of community building as churches were in the main, these cowboys appear to have played no significant role in their establishment, and the churches appear to have played only a social, as opposed to a religious, role in the lives of the cowboys. It is true that Henry Record, for example, was a long-time supporter of both Hardin-Simmons University and the Baptist Childrens' Home at Portales, New Mexico, but the fact that Record is the one former cowboy in this study who had no offspring may have influenced him to seek an agency as his heir. And Eugene H. Price contributed land for, and was a major financial supporter of, the Methodist Church in Lovington, but his father was a Methodist minister, so that heritage no doubt influenced him to a large degree.

These two men notwithstanding, interviews with descendants of the other cowboys suggest that they were not regular church-goers, nor did most ever join an organized religion. Instead, their religious beliefs appear to have been of the "natural" variety that was summed up by the ninety-two year old son of one of the cowboys: "If you done right you were going to be all right when you died."[48] One of the few old open range cowboys who joined a church was Tom Ross—the resident outlaw—only to be "churched" (driven from the fold by consensus of other church members), although his precise offense has not been documented.[49]

In civic duty, religious participation, industry, family patterns, and folkways, the thirty-two cowboys seem to have established communities much like those they were raised in. Earl Pomeroy, one of the first historians to argue for the idea of continuity in western history, observed:

> We may see that conservatism, inheritance, and continuity bulked at least as large in the history of the West as radicalism and environment. The Westerner has been fundamentally imitator rather than innovator.[50]

Today, Jerome O. Steffen and others have strengthened the case for continuity in western traditions.

Traditions appear to have been replicated on a regional scale as well. D. W. Meinig, for example, has suggested that as the West Texas environment filled to its limits, "it was carried beyond the geometrical political boundary to stamp the firm impress of Texas upon a long strip of the borderlands of New Mexico."[51] As stated earlier, many of the Lea County cowboys in this study were from Texas. Quite naturally, Texas traditions were a continuous theme in the lives of the cowboys studied, and today in New Mexico Lea County is known as "Little Texas."[52]

Cultural standardization existed, then, in fraternal organizations, religious institutions, and community and individual folkways and became the norm. To paraphrase Pomeroy, the conservative West did emulate the East.[53] As the open range closed, settlers began to make western communities that looked and acted much the same as those found in older areas of the nation.[54]

But did these communities in Lea County (or elsewhere in the West, for that matter) in any way regard the cowboys who lived there as local heroes, or reward them in any way for having held that occupation?[55] Unequivocally, the answer is no. Working as a cowboy was not the romantic occupation that pulp fiction tried to make it and any aura of past cowboying experience appears to have disappeared on its own or been voluntarily discarded at the first opportunity. Neither community nor individual particularly honored or elevated cowboys over other citizens.

4

Their Fences and Furrows

That cowboys are legendary is indisputable. William W. Savage, Jr. remarks at the outset of *The Cowboy Hero: His Image in American History and Culture* that "as a representative of an occupational group he has received perhaps more attention than any other worker in the history of the world."[1] Not a few of the books written about cowboys emphasize their legendary affinity for their horse. Without a horse, one could argue, there would be no cowboy. The title to one book, *If I Can Do It Horseback,* perhaps typifies the attitude that the horse is what actually separated cowboys from lesser beings;[2] that is, a real cowboy knew his privileged place was on his steed. Other ranch work, such as branding and castrating, done largely on the ground, was considered less desirable than cow work performed on horseback. Some early-day cowboys even demanded a "straight ridin' job."[3]

As late as 1905, one publication for cowboys and cowmen was suggesting that to hold one's place above common earthlings (that is, to retain cowboy status) required uncommon traits:

> Perhaps in no other occupation of men was the theory of
> the "survival of the fittest" more plainly demonstrated in
> practice than in the quick weeding out of the weaklings, of
> the visionary, and of the inherently depraved, among those
> who undertook the cowboy life.[4]

Walt Wiggins wrote this about Horse Walker, one such horse-bound cowboy: "Horse Walker never did like any work he couldn't do horseback. He said he'd rather be caught dead than on the blister end of a shovel."[5]

Not everyone saw a horse as better than a shovel; indeed some modern-day writers, including Don Hedgpeth, noted that "according to the modern prejudices of society, the men who stay in the saddle as working cowhands do so because of a lack of responsibility or initiative."[6] "From sodbuster to cowboy was an easy transition to . . . make,"[7] according to the literature dealing with cowboys. Yet that same literature expresses the notion that to return to farming was a fate worse than death to any genuine cowboy.

For the Lea County cowboys in this study, however, that appears not to have been the case. Each of the thirty-two former open range cowboys took up a homestead. While Billington and others have concluded that the Homestead Act of 1862 played an insignificant role in the settlement of the West[8] and that "a farm of 160 acres was too small to be profitably tilled on the semiarid plains," still Lea County was primarily settled by families taking up 160-acre parcels. Further, many of them attempted to dryland farm and in other ways work the soil.

Sam Cooper's son had this to say about homesteading around Jal in the southern end of Lea County:

> Most every homesteader had come from a farm some-
> where. So each one would clear a patch 30 to 60 acres and
> farm, and would raise a lot of feed three out of five years,
> and some feed every year. The good years you could raise
> corn, maize, cane, etc. I have seen feed grown taller than
> a man's head.[9]

With the farming background that several had, they
were probably aware that the largely inhospitable soil of
the Llano Estacado would not yield the harvests possible
elsewhere. Still they took up shovel and plow and served
their time on the "blister end" of both. Richard Heidel
and "Moster" Lewis became substantial farmers with
large acreages devoted to field crops. An additional
seven cowboys engaged in farming to a degree in combi-
nation with minor stockfarming, and all but three appear
to have personally toiled in gardens large enough to
produce food for their families. Farming was not the
cowboys' only agricultural pursuit; ranching was also a
common pursuit. *(See Figure 5.)*

Eugene Price, one of the cowboys in the primary
study group, wrote of the closing of the open range as the
end of the days when "all a fellow had to do to get into the
ranching business was to sink a well, and put up a
windmill and shack."[10] Price, however, became a considerable landholder and cow*man* from his lowly beginnings as simple cow*boy,* as did nearly a dozen others. His
ability to acquire several sections of grass (and the
similar successes of others) would seem to contradict a

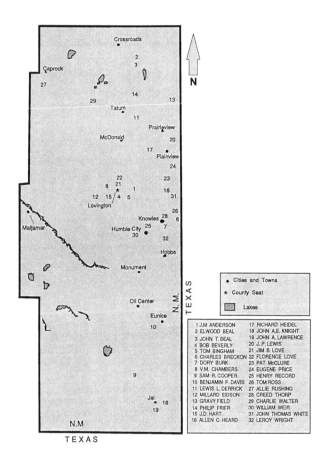

Crossroads

Caprock

27

Tatum

McDonald

Prairieview

Plainview

Lovington

Knowles

Maljamar

Humble City

Hobbs

Monument

Oil Center

Eunice

Jai

N.M

TEXAS

N. M.

TEXAS

• Cities and Towns

★ County Seat

▨ Lakes

1 J.M ANDERSON	17 RICHARD HEIDEL
2 ELWOOD BEAL	18 JOHN A.E. KNIGHT
3 JOHN T. BEAL	19 JOHN A. LAWRENCE
4 BOB BEVERLY	20 J. P. LEWIS
5 TOM BINGHAM	21 JIM B. LOVE
6 CHARLES BRECKON	22 FLORENCE LOVE
7 DORY BURK	23 PAT McCLURE
8 V.M. CHAMBERS	24 EUGENE PRICE
9 SAM R. COOPER	25 HENRY RECORD
10 BENJAMIN F. DAVIS	26 TOM ROSS
11 LEWIS L. DERRICK	27 ALLIE RUSHING
12 MILLARD EIDSON	28 CREED THORP
13 GRAVY FIELD	29 CHARLIE WALTER
14 PHILIP FRIER	30 WILLIAM WEIR
15 J.D. HART	31 JOHN THOMAS WHITE
16 ALLEN C. HEARD	32 LEROY WRIGHT

Figure 5. Approximate Homestead and Ranching Locations of the Thirty-two Cowboys in the Primary Study Group

belief held by many that rarely were cowboys able to rise above the common laboring class or amass any excess capital or own land.[11] In all, ten of the thirty-two cowboys studied managed to put together sizable holdings: John T. Beal, V. M. Chambers, Millard Eidson, "Gravy" Field, Allen C. Heard, "Moster" Lewis, Eugene Price, Henry Record, William Weir, and Tom T-Bar White.

Several of the cowboys who later became ranchers in Lea County got their start while still working as cowboys. Eugene Price recounts a practice of George Littlefield, noted rancher:

> An admirable characteristic of the LFD people was their willingness to let the boys whom they worked as regular hands have a brand of their own and run it on LFD range free of charge until they acquired as many as three or four hundred cattle at which time they were usually asked to put down a watering place.[12]

The cowboys under study here both farmed and ranched successfully, and they entered other occupations with varying degrees of success. What appears to have provided the overriding direction for these successes, however, probably had less to do with the desire to either farm or avoid farming, and more to do with opportunity and a search for "economic independence."[13]

The cowboys here who eventually became cowmen did so by a variety of means, all based upon seizing opportunities as they arose. Millard Eidson formed a partnership with John Scharbauer of West Texas ranching fame; several, like Henry Record and "Gravy" Field, were frugal to the extent that they were able to buy out unsuccessful homesteaders; some worked for open range outfits that allowed them to accumulate cattle of their own; and most were wise enough to retain the mineral rights on properties they had homesteaded, thereby becoming financially successful through oil and gas production.

Almost everywhere, but especially in the West, owning land was perceived as the means to secure economic independence. According to many homesteaders interviewed, more than 90 percent of those who settled the eastern side of New Mexico commencing about 1905 were "looking for land."[14] In Lea County, Samuel Theodore "Dory" Burk typifies these homesteaders. Burk left home at the age of eight after a fight with another boy. After his mother's death when he was seventeen, he never went back to his home in Denton County, Texas. When he came to Lea County, he was "still seeking that bit of land to call his own."[15]

The Llano Estacado of eastern New Mexico was parcelled out as part of the 80 million acres homesteaded after 1862 in the West, and the Lea County cowboys, like many other western homesteaders, became landowners of plots too small to provide subsistence as ranches and too dry to provide subsistence as farms.[16] Still, evidence suggests that the desire for economic independence via land acquisition practiced by the open range cowboys may have been predictable. Henry Harrison Campbell, who managed the hugely successful Matador Land and Cattle Company, urged his cowboys to make themselves useful and law-abiding citizens in the country they had pioneered . . . [and] to take advantage of the liberal land laws, acquire property, and thus provide for their future.[17]

Charles Goodnight's rhetorical question summed up the views many in Lea County held about the importance of owning land: "[D]id anybody ever hear of any country being anything where the people did not own the soil? Properties of no kind can be safe where the people are not fixed to the land."[18]

The countryside in which the former open range cowboys lived was peopled with like-minded individuals; that is, people primarily making their livelihood from the land. For example, in the community of Lovington at the taking of the federal decennial census in 1910, there were 285 families enumerated. From among those 285 units, there were 324 individuals old enough to be engaged in some form of agricultural pursuit as an occupation. Of those 324 men (and women), 161, or 49 percent, were engaged in farming.[19] These figures are at odds with the notion that the land was totally unsuited to agriculture.

Ten of the thirty-two cowboys studied became major ranchers, holding ten sections or more.[20] Another seven cowboys acquired from five to ten sections. Four from this total of seventeen landholders acquired enough land to make them wealthy.[21]

Robert Athearn has suggested that the men who took up farming or stockfarming had no choice: the huge open range outfits had passed and the cattle barons were gone. Those who had previously considered themselves cowboys had no choice but "to join the common folk as stock raisers."[22] But there is no evidence that the cowboys here regretted the fact that they became stock farmers.

Moreover, they appear to have made the choice to become family men freely and appear not to have spoken often of their cowboy past nor dwelt upon missed opportunities or diminished personal freedom. On the contrary, they appear to have been of one mind to seize opportunities presented them. They looked to the future not the past. The thirty-two cowboys married, fathered a total of 125 children, and became, in the main, substantial and responsible citizens.

It has been shown, then, that the occupational group called *cowboy* had no greater or lesser impact upon these men collectively than any other occupation would have had. They made a smooth transition from farm background to cowboy, and the transition from cowboy back to farming, ranching, and other pursuits was made just as smoothly. This suggests that when a factory or place of employment closes, one simply moves on to another venue and works at another trade, cowboy lamentations in folksongs notwithstanding.

5

Trail's End, Myth's End

"The West is the loveliest and most enduring of our myths, and the only one that has been universally accepted."[1] Undeniably, the cowboy is the most salient character to emerge from American history. Ironically, that the cowboy myth "exists in fact...[makes it] a more influential social force than the actual cowboy ever was." In William Savage's hyperbolic suggestion, cowboys belong "somewhere above the President and below Christ."[2] Popular literature, under the pen of Ned Buntline, Owen Wister, and countless other writers, created a cowboy culture nearly devoid of fact, but their tales were credible to readers because, as literary creations, they served a public curious about the frontier they themselves might never see.[3]

One myth is that a cowboy preferred being outdoors in the wide open spaces doing what he loved best; at least one Lea County cowboy, however, does not fit well with this myth. V. M. Chambers found his cowboying work "a trial"; he did not like being out in inclement weather, and "began to think of what he could do which did not involve the weather." In an opportunity seized, Chambers (who had only a second grade education at that time) passed by a schoolhouse, and decided he would go back to school. He was twenty-two years old when he largely abandoned the cowboy life.[4]

Unquestionably, Americans in the late nineteenth century were curious about the various frontiers beyond their front yards. But what is less understandable is why it was the cowboy—the common laborer of the frontier—who was chosen as the western hero.

> It is curious that of all the possible occupational types to choose from that played a role in the white history of the West, it was the cowboy that emerged as the most romantic Western figure. Here was a man, quite often a boy, whose time was routinely spent on a horse—riding line, rounding up cattle, eating dust, and earning twenty-five to forty dollars a month which was usually spent in town carousing with prostitutes—a man who for a living castrated animals and placed a red hot iron on the hindquarters of cattle to sear into its flesh a brand used for identification. It is difficult to find any trace of the romantic in the actual work of a cowboy.[5]

But it was found romantic, or at least the version depicted in popular writing became so. The Western hero— "born in print in the 1830s . . . ," reborn in film at the turn of the century, and recreated as a staple of television[6]—in all its presentations became what one writer has called a "product of a particular industry in a specific environment."[7] Despite the fabrications surrounding the cowboy, Joe B. Frantz and Julian Choate contend that the myth is "fundamental to an understanding of the cultural content of American life." [8]

With respect to national character, Thomas Hartshorne has written that "any collection of people which is not fortuitous and random is distinguished by certain characteristics that permit the ready identification of the group as a group."[9] But he also points out that some of the stereotypes of American national character are more nearly "national caricature," for they "select, emphasize, and exaggerate certain elements."[10] That the caricature would prevail was foreseen, interestingly, by Cordelia Sloan Duke, whose husband controlled the mighty XIT ranching empire. She predicted that cowboys would be "glamorized and the memory of their work distorted by writers who could sense a pay vein when they saw one."[11] Several of the thirty-two Lea County cowboys worked for the famed XIT, yet failed to record that fact or stress it sufficiently to their descendants. They omitted entirely their work experience on the XIT range in family reminiscences.

Popular history has also created myths about cowboys, and some cowboys have created them as well. J. Frank Dobie (who had a flair for the dramatic himself) wrote, "The average old-timer of open range days put himself wherever possible, and often where not possible, into Indian fights and stampedes and strained his memory to be an eyewitness to badman exploits."[12]

Tall tales abound in the writings by some cowboys. For example, among those early-day cowboys who purported to describe the reality of the Old West was Charles Siringo; however, within the last decade, Siringo has been dubbed, and rightly, "an unreliable fabulist."[13]

Such writings appeared on the local scene as well. Beyond the yen to be an eyewitness was the braggadocio attitude expressed by Bob Beverly, who has been quoted as saying that "a cowboy who couldn't wear his name out and take on a new one in six months was not to be depended upon." Beverly could spin a yarn as well as the next man and did so for many years. But his tale-telling must be viewed as a way of satisfying his readership, for away from his stories he was a stable and reliable man.[14]

Also suspect as a generalization is this claim by J. Frank Dobie about cowboys: "Men who work hard out in the open generally lead straight lives."[15] So, literature has tended to err on both sides, painting the cowboy as either plodding or heroic. In truth, since he was nothing if not a typical young man of the times, he must have fallen somewhere between hero and clod, as did most working-class Americans of the late nineteenth century. While it may appear unkind to portray cowboys as a "class of men almost wholly without historical significance,"[16] that is what they were—as a class. But that is what *any* similar occupational group would have been, which is to say that while as *individuals* they may have been remarkable or outstanding human beings, their occupational group was uniformly unremarkable in what it added to the stream of American history. Scholars admonish students of western history to approach the field as "the study of people as problem solvers who attempted to gain maximum political and economic success while maintaining intellectual and social stability."[17] It is in searching out such roles—rather than for what some term a "faddish" interest[18]—that it is important to study cowboys as an occupational group, as components of western communities, as social and political beings, and as problem solvers. The myths generally associated with cowboys (and the literature about them,[19] in the main) have not contributed significantly to such a historical study. Worse, the myths have been counterproductive to a unified, scholarly interest in Western history.

What emerges from studying the former open range cowboys who eventually settled in present-day Lea County, New Mexico, is that their actions and words refute nearly every cowboy myth. One exception may be Dory Burk's claim to be a balladeer on the cattle trails who frequently traded off his night watch to sing for the others around the campfire.[20] This certainly is illustrative of synchronization with cowboy myth.

Among the cowboys studied here the transition from farmer to cowboy and back to farmer or other common occupations occurred apparently without trauma. This is in contrast to one cowboy myth—that cowboys yearned to do their work and were melancholy when not atop a horse.[21] This study suggests that there may have been several reasons why young men left home to take up range work. But what seems clear is that they probably did not do that because they thought it would bring them a romantic and adventurous career. "Like most other wage-earners . . . [a cowboy] works because he must work in order to live, and not for the joy of the thing he does."[22] Cow work, of course, is not glamorous, as has been demonstrated elsewhere in this book.

Another myth about cowboys is that they were all vagabonds, marginal characters, and irresponsible bullies. But Skaggs points out in *Cattle-Trailing* that they "seldom carried a gun, apparently never shot anyone, and rarely romanticized about their own contribution."[23] While it has not been documented how many of the cowboys in this study carried a gun while on the trail, several were later involved in scrapes with the law. Yet these incidents appear not to have had anything to do with the fact that they were ex-cowboys.

Atherton has suggested that the "average American cowboy" didn't care about financial success,[24] but the cowboys of this study do not fit that mold. To a man, they appear to have been ambitious, even aggressive, in seeking economic independence. With the unique geography of the Llano Estacado and oil as an economic multiplier, several experienced great financial success,[25] while perhaps still claiming, as Henry Record did, that "he hated the smell of oil and so did his cows."[26]

Views of cowboying as an occupation have distorted reality. At one level, for example, is the opinion of one of the stockholders of the Mallet Company who lived in New England and knew nothing about ranching. After he watched a long day's work on a rare visit to the Staked Plains, he commented: "The cowboy life is just one continual round of pleasure."[27] Another example of a view by an outsider comes from letters written by a young woman visiting Roswell, New Mexico:

There are many hotels here and a wholesale grocery larger than anything at home, but things are so awfully expensive. . . . The principal things down here are cattle and cowboys and I haven't met any cowboys yet.[28]

The young woman, in another letter, illustrates an outsider's intense interest in the West:

Last Sunday I got a box of things from home and *my* how glad I was. There were several new books, among other things, including two about the west—"A Texas Cowboy" by Siringo and "Over the Range" by Emerson Hough.[29]

Another problem associated with cowboy mythology is what Parks terms "reality versus art (or artifice)."[30] In the case of the cowboy, it appears that it was "life imitating art imitating life," which is to say that when young cowboys sought role models, they took them not from real cowboys but from the imitation cowboys of pulp fiction and Hollywood. This is an interesting phenomenon since they were surrounded by *real* cowboys and were, themselves, working cowboys. For example, one cowboy quoted in *The Mythic West in Twentieth Century America,* said, "I learned to 'build me a smoke'— rolled Bull Durham—one that drooped properly from my lips in the manner I had seen cowboys use on the movie screen."[31] Another more contemporary article cites the "amusing spectacle of a youthful cowboy becoming so enamored of the kind of 'punchers' pictured in modern fiction that he purchases a pair of utterly useless sixshooters, commences to walk with a swagger, and to imitate the dialect of Red Saunders."[32]

Still others tell of "hired hands—the cowboys—spending hours in the bunkhouse reading Beadle pulps and attempting to imitate the cowboy heroes depicted therein."[33] If the open range cowboys of this study engaged in such theatrics, it has not been discovered.

And what about the cowboy reunions? While their purpose was probably not to reminisce about their work as cowboys but rather to renew old friendships, at least one writer has suggested that the get-togethers served to turn "humdrum fact into fascinating fiction."[34] And in a way, the Open Range Cowboys Association meetings held in Lea County contribute to this phenomena, for hundreds of people attend the annual fête on the second Saturday in September. Each participant claims descent from an open range cowboy, thus recreating a little piece of mythical Americana. Each erroneously believes that his or her father or grandfather helped "win the West," when it is questionable to suggest that any common laborer, cowboy included, played much of a role in the settlement of the West. As cowmen, they had a place perhaps; but not as cowboys. Each believes that his ancestor was born to the saddle and was a cowboy until he died. Each believes that cowboy myth—that particular myth—that has been tightly woven into our American psyche.

Appendix A

Biographical Data, Cowboys in Primary Study Group

J. S. "Jim" Anderson, born 1872, Murray County, Georgia; died 1930; married in 1896; four children. In 1888 the family moved to Texas, settling in Kyle County and later moving to Childress. According to a family source, Anderson began working as a cowboy not long after the Texas move, at which time he  would have been close to eighteen years old. Anderson moved from Petersburg, Texas, to Lea County in 1906 and settled in a dry lake about four miles east of the present site of Lovington. He reportedly had an open range operation in Lea until about 1915, by which time the local ranchers finally fenced their land. Anderson worked for the XIT, and his name is among their former cowboys in a 1939 reunion booklet. It is interesting that Anderson's family never mentioned his XIT days when writing about his life.[1]

Elwood Beal, born 1860, at Sweetwater, Texas, in that portion of the old Territory of Young that later became Nolan County; died c. 1915; married in 1903; one child. From about the age of sixteen, Elwood was employed by various outfits near San Angelo, Water Valley, Gail, and Lubbock. Then he helped drive the first herd of John Turner Beal's cattle from Milam County to Borden County, Texas, in 1879. Later on, he worked for Beal on other ranches, including Beal's outfit near Ranger Lake in present-day Lea County, New Mexico. While making a trip from Elida to his homestead in the Ranger Lake area, he was struck by lightning and killed. Three of his four mules were also killed, but his wife and young son, who were riding in the wagon to get out of the rain during the storm, were spared.[2]

John Turner Beal, born 1848, Milam County, Texas; died 1916; married in 1900; three children. Beal began cow work at the age of twelve. Beginning in 1866, Beal and a partner freighted and herded cattle, making three trips up the Chisholm Trail to Abilene,

Kansas, and two trips to St. Louis, the latter with his own cattle. He saved funds to purchase the Jumbo Cattle Company with fenced pastures in Garza, Borden, Cochran, Kent, and Scurry counties in Texas; later he purchased an interest in the St. Louis Cattle Company in Cochran and Crosby counties, Texas, holding 15,000 head of cattle. In 1891, looking for grass and water, he moved into the Ranger Lake area of present-day Lea County.[3]

Bob Beverly, born 1872, Ringold, Georgia; died 1958; married five times; five children; two of his marriages ended in divorce. Orphaned at age twelve, Beverly drifted to the Wichita ranges and Indian Territory where he spent time "hanging with outlaws." He drifted on "until he found friendly faces among the cowboys taking in the gambling places and saloons of the little cowtown of Midland in West Texas." In 1890 as an eighteen-

year-old cowboy, he worked for the 69 Ranch and later "drove the Texas-Montana cattle trail," worked for the XIT Ranch, punched cows in the Comstock country along the Rio Grande, worked for Slaughter's Long S, and for the Quien Sabe. Later, he worked as wagon boss for the JAL. He served as sheriff and tax collector for Midland County, 1909-1912. From 1916 to 1921 he was cattle inspector for the Texas and Southwestern Cattle Raisers Association; 1923-1930, brand inspector for Lea County, New Mexico; 1933-1937, sheriff of Lea County.[4]

Tom Bingham, born 1872, Italy, Ellis County, Texas; died 1944; married in 1906; six children. Bingham began range work at the age of twelve as a trail driver for cattle moving out of Texas. He came to Lea County in 1906, working for the Poole Cattle Company while proving up on his claim. Bingham served as the Lea County tax assessor for two terms commencing in 1922, as a justice of the peace, as the first probate judge of Lea County, and as deputy sheriff at Hobbs and later at Tatum, New Mexico.[5]

Charles Michael Breckon, born 1854, New York; died 1920; married in 1875; five children. Breckon came west at the age of fourteen and "joined roaming cowboys," worked on various ranches in Texas, and participated in several drives to Kansas. Still later, Breckon worked for the Bronson, the Hat, and the 84 ranches. While on a "cow hunt" in Palo Pinto County, Texas, at the age of

twenty-one, he married. During his cowboy days, he made two trips up the Chisholm Trail. He came to Lea County first in 1884, settling near the old Nadine community, but went back to the Midland area. He took up another site in Lea County in 1898 and a third in 1900, just east of present-day Hobbs near the state line. He ranched, drilled water wells, and worked as a wagon boss for the JAL.[6]

Samuel Theodore (Dory) Burk, born 1870, Denton County, Texas; died 1968; married in 1897; five children. Burk left home at the age of eight after a fight with another boy. He hired out to a Denton area family for room and board. His mother died when he was seventeen, but he had only "appeared and reappeared" in his family's life to that time. After his mother's death, he never went back home. His first cowboy job was for the Clint Riders' outfit when he was nine. At eighteen, he worked his way to Wise County, driving herds to Quanah, by which time he was a "seasoned veteran." In 1893 he went up the trail with 5,000 head to Miles City, Montana, with the XIT outfit. Later he worked for OX Land and Cattle, was a constable, butcher, and railroad worker. Burk came to Lea County in 1909.[7]

V. M. Chambers, born 1868, Collin County, Texas; died 1957; married in 1912; two children. In 1890 Chambers was "trailing cattle to the Indian Territory" to winter. During the next decade he worked his way back and forth across Texas and across the New Mexico territorial line spending the winter and spring breaking

horses for various ranches. He located in Lea County permanently in 1920, where he became a large sheep rancher.[8]

Sam R. Cooper, born 1874, Kansas; died 1958; married in 1901; eight children. Cooper's father had owned a wagon yard, which may account for the fact that for most of his adult life he worked as a freighter and had large teams of mules. Cooper, from about the age of eighteen, worked for the XIT, and he was listed in their 1939 reunion booklet. He moved to Lea County in 1914 from Wheeler County, Texas, where his residence was listed as Cooper, New Mexico (a community named for his parents). A fairly extensive write-up about Cooper's life was detailed by his son, but no mention was made of his XIT days or any other cowboy work. His son did concede that he was "more of a freighter than a farmer or rancher." [9]

Benjamin Franklin Davis, born 1843, South Carolina; died 1934; married in 1882; seven children. After the Civil War, he came with his sisters to Texas. He "helped drive one herd over the Chisholm Trail," and worked cattle on the Brazos in Bosque County, Texas. Later he served as a deputy sheriff in Paint Rock, Texas, and as a cattle inspector, member of the commissioner's court, and later as sheriff. He came to present-day Lea County in 1909 and "bought the improvements on a so-called ranch."[10]

Lewis L. Derrick, born 1863, Lamar County, Texas; died 1954; married c. 1893; four children. Derrick was hired as a cowboy at about age sixteen; he worked for the XIT (and was included in their 1939 reunion booklet). He also was foreman of the Witherspoon Land and Cattle Company near Ft. Sumner, New Mexico, on the east side of the state. He moved permanently to New Mexico in 1912, homesteading five miles east of Tatum. According to his off-spring, "Dad farmed as little as possible, since he left Texas to get away from the plowed up pasture land." A newspaper clipping pictures Derrick at a Prairieview oldtimers' gathering at age eighty-nine with the caption, "The Sage of Tatum." He lived to be ninety-one years old.[11]

Millard Eidson, born 1874, Missouri; died 1966; married in 1909; one child. He was a teenager when he began working cattle, first coming to Lea County in 1894. He landed a job with Pemberton and Connell as their windmill man, but he "pro-gressed to a much better job." His associa-tion with that outfit led to his life-long partnership with the Scharbauer Cattle Company of Midland, Texas, and by 1940, "he bought out John Scharbauer," one of West Texas' largest ranchers. Eidson served as a Gaines County, Texas, commissioner, 1905–1907. The family lived in Midland, Texas, until 1927, then moved into Lea County and began acquiring ranches. Eidson was a prominent and influential Lea County rancher.[12]

Herschel Robert "Gravy" Field, born 1874, Batesville, Ar-kansas; died 1942; married in 1909; three children. Field's family moved to the Jacksboro, Texas, area when he was quite small. According to a family member, he knew early on that he did not want

to spend time behind a plow as his father had, so he began to hang around cow camps, picking up cow chips or generally making himself useful at whatever tasks a young boy could handle. He came to the Bronco area of Lea County in 1901 and started the 07 Ranch, which then as now was one of the larger ranches in the area. His cowboy work began in 1889 with the XIT Ranch. Family members state that he was with the XIT through 1891, but another source claims that he was "on the trail for the XIT" in the spring of 1892. On his second trip to New Mexico he stayed, married, and settled down. Field accumulated a great deal of property by buying out homesteaders who gave up on their claims.[13]

Philip Frier, born 1870, Hill County, Texas; died 1938; married in 1907; four children. His father died when he was young, so he left home at the age of twelve to begin herding cattle. As a young man he worked for the F Ranch near the Matador and later wrangled horses and broke broncs for the LFD. He came to Lea County in 1901, taking up a homestead. He ran cattle, but for a number of years Frier was also a sheep rancher.[14]

Jefferson D. Hart, born 1861, Jacksboro, Texas; died 1948; married in 1911; three children. What he did before 1884 is not known, but Hart worked as a cowboy from the age of twenty-three. Making several drives up the Pecos River, he eventually became a Bar V man on the Pecos, but "quit them to work for LFDs because he had a better show to get somewhere." He was wagon boss for the LFD, coming first to present-day Lea County in 1888.[15]

Allen Clinton Heard, born 1858, DeWitt County, Texas; died 1944; married in 1887; two children. Heard spent his younger days as a ranch employee in south Texas, and he worked his way up to trail boss from drives into Kansas. His last job for salary was manager of the N. B. Pulliam Ranch in Pecos County, Texas, in 1887. In that year he pooled his resources with Tom (T-Bar) White and they "got into the game as cattle owners in the country south of Midland not too far from the San Angelo country." In 1887 they purchased the Mallet Ranch in Lea County, naming it the Highlonesome after a previous ranch in Texas.[16]

Richard Heidel, born 1881, Germany, died 1954; married in 1906; four children. Heidel was thirteen years old when his father, who had immigrated in 1883, died. Heidel immediately struck out on his own as a cowboy working north from Austin. About 1894 he worked for the XIT Ranch helping survey for fences, scouting for expansion possibilities, and wrangling horses. It was on a scouting expedition that he first glimpsed the New Mexico side of the line, settling permanently in Lea County in 1910. Heidel's daughter claims "cowboying" was "all he knew to do," but in later years he made his living as a farmer. When applying for United States citizenship (in order that he might prove up on his claim), one story claims Heidel met some resistance with the bureaucrats in Roswell, which was settled to his satisfaction when a man shoved a .45 pistol into his hip pocket and said, "Smoke them out, Heidel."[17]

John Ambrose Ellis Knight, Jr., born 1866, Indian Territory; died 1927; married in 1890; four children. Often called Captain, Knight was the son of an adventurer who went west on the Oregon Trail then found his way back to the Choctaw Nation. Knight was a scout and wagon master who made "many trips from California to Missouri," and who later "drove cattle from Texas to Kansas." Still later, after he homesteaded in Lea County, he worked as a carpenter.[18]

John Albert Lawrence, born 1846, Alabama; died 1916; married in 1871; eleven children. Lawrence began working as a cowboy in 1870 when he was twenty-four years old. He came from Alabama to Texas first as a scout for a wagon train and, after his marriage, he made cattle drives to Kansas from Henderson County, Texas, until 1876. Then he leased land in Brown County, Texas, and ran his own cattle on open grass on the Colorado River. After four drives into New Mexico Territory, he settled his family in the south end of present-day Lea County. His family claims it was he who sold his J A L brand to the Cowden brothers who then operated the JAL Ranch. The area around the present site of Jal, New Mexico, however, was not to Mrs. Lawrence's liking and she demanded they leave. About the same time all his horses ate locoweed and went crazy or died. The family, after no more than an eighteen-month stay in Lea County, moved to Coleman County, Texas. Previous to this claim, historians have generally concluded that it was John A. Lynch who sold his brand to the Cowdens and had the town of Jal named for that outfit.[19]

John Parish "Moster" Lewis, born 1865, Tennessee; died 1939; married in 1881; four children. Lewis began working on ranches at an early age: the Cross C, the XIT, and the Matador were reportedly some of them. By the 1880s he was a windmill man for the LFD Ranch. He established his own ranch, which he held continually, though not always in residence, from 1894 until his death. Lewis later farmed and one hobby was gardening. He also took "occasional trips to Kansas City on drunks" with the doctor from a neighboring community.[20]

James Benjamin Love, born 1873, Palo Pinto County, Texas; died 1945; married twice, second in 1903; seven children. As a seventeen-year-old cowboy, Jim Love worked his way west to the New Mexico Territory line in 1891. In 1892 he worked for the Matador Ranch. In succeeding years he did cow work for the Mallet, the Tule, and the JA at Palo Duro. One cattle drive to Montana was made with a Matador herd. In the late 1890s, he worked for the E Ranch, formerly the Ink Bar, in the neighborhood of present-day Lea County. In 1902 he worked for the Hat Ranch and for other smaller operators. In 1906 he filed on a claim at the present site of Lovington. Love's daughter has stated, "Papa was proud to be a cowboy and considered himself one all his life," but he held any number of occupations alien to a ranch life: restauranteur, pool hall and domino parlor operator, hotel proprietor, ice cream and confectionery store owner, mail service car operator, and oilfield worker.[21]

Robert Florence Love, born 1870, Palo Pinto County, Texas; died 1943; married in 1896; four children. Both this first and a subsequent marriage ended in divorce. Florence Love worked as a cowboy for his father-in-law near Stanton, Texas, for about four years; then in 1891 he worked for the Ink Bar (Pemberton and Connell's E Ranch) and for the Mallet in 1892. That same year he and his brother drove a herd of cattle to Colorado City, Texas, for the Mallets. Love had apparently first been as far west as the New Mexico line about 1890 when he was moving cattle to Plains, Texas; then in 1900 he

settled permanently in Lea County. He appears to have lived his last years as a day laborer on area ranches while running a few head of his own cattle.[22]

Pat McClure, born 1872, Jack County, Texas; died 1957; married in 1897; eight children. He worked for the XIT, the Spade Ranch, Pat McQue, and various other outfits from the "Canadian River south to the Texas and Pacific Railway" from about the age of seventeen. (He is listed in the 1939 XIT reunion booklet.) According to one of McClure's daughters, "my dad worked for different cowmen or whatever he could find to

do." The family moved to Lea County from Palo Pinto County, Texas, in 1909, but "starved out" and went back to Texas for awhile. McClure had a small farm and served on the Prairieview school board. One of his sons became a cowboy of a different sort—world champion calf roper Jake McClure.[23]

Eugene H. Price, born 1868, Grayson County, Texas; died 1952; married in 1889; nine children. His work began about 1890 for the Quinn Brothers operation on Sulfur Draw near Plains, Texas. In 1892 he went, representing the LFDs, to Slaughter's Long S Ranch for pool work. Price was with Quinn until 1897 when he went to work for Pemberton and Connell on the E Ranch. "I took my little bunch of cattle over there," Price has said, which was typical of what was then allowed on some open range ranches in West Texas and

Southeastern New Mexico. With seven others, Price founded the First National Bank at Lovington. He left Lovington about 1930 and ranched near Santa Rosa, New Mexico, until his death.[24]

Henry Record, born 1872, Palo Pinto County, Texas; died 1962; married in 1898; no children. Henry Record came to West Texas to work for the Cowden's operation in 1890; he also worked for the Muleshoe Ranch and for an outfit on the Pecos River. A fellow cowboy wrote that Record roamed "to the Colorado River country and up by Big Spring and the Midland Country, northwest back to the line of Texas" working as a cowboy. In 1897 Record started his own cow outfit, proved up on a homestead, and worked as a wagon boss for the pool wagon early in the twentieth century in Lea County. Record was an eccentric individual who, during his long ranching career, amassed a considerable

fortune by, in his words, two means: "I'd been getting twenty-five a month and buying heifers with it," and "as settlers moved off I bought 'em out."[25]

Tom Ross, born Hillary U. Loftis, 1872, Mississippi; died 1929; married in 1904; one child. Ross appears to have begun as a cowboy at about the age of thirteen when he left home and never returned. As a young man he reportedly was a member of the Red Buck Gang, which rustled cattle and robbed banks along the Canadian River in Texas and in Indian Territory. By the fall of 1889 he was working on the W. T. Waggoner Ranch in north central Texas. In 1892 he filed on four sections in Gaines County where he would eventually make his home, but his cattle operation in this century crossed the line into New Mexico Territory near the community of Knowles. Further, he had many business and personal dealings in Lea County and was well known in Lea, making him a candidate for this study. Fenton has fully described Ross's numerous brushes with lawlessness, including the murder of two men in Seminole, Texas, just a few miles from his home. Aimless drifting

may have characterized his life, as Fenton contends, but his ties to Lea County resulted in his becoming a local legend.[26]

Alfred Green Rushing, born 1876, Louisiana; died 1953; married in 1903; seven children. Allie Rushing was known as the best chuckwagon cook on the Llano Estacado, working primarily for the Hat Ranch. Both his parents died when he was young, so he left Louisiana to work as a cowboy in Texas at the age of fourteen. On first coming west, he wrangled horses. Then "one day the chuckwagon cook quit," sealing Rushing's cowboy fate. He filed on a homestead at Salt Lake, Eddy County, then moved to the Pearl community in Lea County, where he helped organize the first

school. He served as a county commissioner, but in 1923 conditions "forced him to sell his holdings and go back to cooking for area ranches." Late in life he bought the Caprock store and ran the post office there until he died.[27]

Creed Thorp, born 1868 in the old Territory of Bexar that later became Concho County, Texas; died 1944; married in 1896;

eleven children. Thorp's father was killed when Thorp was young, and his cowboy work began at the age of about fourteen when he wrangled horses for the LFD Ranch. There he helped "Nigger Ad," Lea County's only well-known black cowboy (see Appendix B). He made cattle drives from south Texas and from north of Austin to Kansas with large herds. He helped trail one herd of 5,000 head to Montana, spending "more than a year on the whole trip" about 1890. Thorp filed on a Lea County homestead in 1902, actually settling on the place in 1904. In later life he freighted for a living and ran a small cattle operation of his own.[28]

Charlie Walter, born 1872, Germany, died 1956; married in 1910; four children. Walter's parents immigrated when he was twelve years old, settling first in Terre Haute, Indiana. Charlie came west when he was thirteen, living with relatives, and working as a sheep herder near Odessa, Texas. He worked for the T Bar X and for Benson Cattle Company. He also reportedly participated in several cattle drives that began on the Pecos River, trailing the herds to Kansas. Walter eventually settled near the town of Eddy (now Carlsbad) in Eddy County, then married. In 1922 he moved to the Nadine community in Lea County, later settling in the area of Caprock in Lea.[29]

William Fletcher Weir, born 1844, Missouri; died 1935; married in 1881; eight children. Weir appears to have made two cattle drives. One was when he "joined Captain Luddell on a trail drive to Abilene," and the other was when he worked "on the trail to Dodge City with a herd of Schriner steers." By 1885, Weir was a young Texas Ranger on the trail of Indians who had stolen horses. The chase brought Weir into New Mexico Territory at Monument Springs, then being operated as the Hat Ranch. According to tradition, Weir vowed then that someday he would own that ranch. He moved his family from

Garden City, Texas, to the springs in 1906 and purchased the Hat.[30]

John Thomas (T-Bar) White, born 1868, Collin County, Texas; died 1926; married in 1894; one child. T-Bar White, so called because of his livestock brand, spent his younger days as a ranch employee for several outfits in south Texas and later "got into the game" as a cattle owner around Midland and San Angelo. It was while he was working as a cowboy in the San Angelo, Texas, area that he met Allen C. Heard, and together they formed the Highlonesome open range outfit in present-day Lea County. White also kept a home in Midland, Texas, where his family lived most of the time. He sold out in 1908 and moved his cattle to the former LFD range then to Gaines County, Texas. White's operation

appears to have been one of the last to be fenced, holding off until 1915.[31]

Leroy Wright, born 1876, Ellis County, Texas; died 1923; married in 1910; four children. Wright appears to have had a privileged background; his ancestors founded Milford, county seat of Ellis. Wright attended Add-Ran College (forerunner of Texas Christian University), after which he came west with his family, working for several years around Quitaque in the Texas panhandle. In 1903 he homesteaded in New Mexico and took up four sections adjoining that claim in Gaines County, Texas. Wright died at the age of forty-six, leaving his widow with four small children. He has been characterized as "witty and bright," with a dry sense of humor, which may

Appendix A

account for the fact that the only existing photograph of him pictures him in bib overalls rather than more stereotypical cowboy attire.[32]

Midland, Texas, c. 1880s. The cowboys pictured include Allen Clinton Heard and Tom T-Bar White, plus an unidentified black cowboy.

Appendix B

Biographical Data on Cowboys Not Included in Primary Study Group

Ben (C-Hop) Baker was with George Littlefield "driving longhorns to Kansas," and is also reported to have "spent so many years with the Jingle Bob (Chisum) outfit on the Pecos River." When Chisum "closed out," Baker went to work for the LFDs. Later he was wagon boss for the Highlonesome. Baker was one of the open range cowboys who did not "marry or have a nice home," but did retire to "a little ranch of his own with several hundred cattle." At least as late as 1915 he was in the Caprock, Lea County, New Mexico, area.[1]

Pat Brady (called "Uncle Pat Brady") was a bachelor who some say was a legend in southeastern New Mexico. He was from Illinois and came west when railroads were being built. After staying in Lincoln County for a time, he drifted to present-day Lea County where he worked for the Hat Ranch, c. 1884. According to one source, "Brady worked for many years as a janitor and furnace man at the bank, where he lived in the basement." Brady was reportedly the oldest cowboy at the 1938 meeting of the Open Range Cowboys in Lovington, and he died shortly afterward.[2]

Lod Callahan was among the first wagon bosses hired by Heard and White at the old Highlonesome Ranch. He quit them to take a job as cattle inspector for the Texas and Southwestern Cattle Raisers Association at the stock yards in Kansas City, Missouri, a job which he held more than thirty years until his death.[3]

Shorty Carrington was a wagon boss at the Highlonesome Ranch for many years, including the year 1889. This cowboy was variously known as Tom Carrington and Eugene Clark, though no reason for the aliases has been discovered.[4]

Jim M. Cook was apparently an unsuccessful open range cowboy for the Hat Ranch, a position from which he was "fired." He stayed in the area, opening a general store in his house. This small beginning became the town of Monument, Lea County, New Mexico. He also had a small post office at his home.[5]

Henry Cummins was a cowboy who worked for Frank Divers at the TAX or Dug Springs Ranch, which later became the San Simon Ranch. He evidently prospered until he was able to buy a one-sixth interest in the TAX, and in 1892 he sold his interest back to Divers.[6]

Addison Jones, or Old Nigger Ad as he was affectionately called, is the only black cowboy documented in Lea County records, although there were vague references to other blacks. That his real name was Addison Jones is a fact not well known among his contemporaries and known by few people since that time. One source suggests he had been with George Littlefield "since emancipation." Another source states that he was "with [George] Causey in Texas" then with Causey "for most of the fifteen years that Causey owned the ranch," then with Littlefield's LFD outfit at Four Lakes in Lea County. In his declining years Jones lived at Roswell, where he reportedly died and is buried.[7]

Johnnie Jones from Arizona was at the Hat Ranch about 1902.[8]

Slosh Jones worked for the Hat Ranch, and has been documented there about 1902.[9]

Spence Jowell was a boss of the pool outfit for the JALs, and described elsewhere as the man who "ran things" for that same ranch. The JAL Ranch was owned by the Cowden Brothers, and Jowell was reportedly their nephew. He is known to have married, had at least three children, and was still living in 1904.[10]

Dink Logan was born in Hill County, Texas, and he was a cowboy who never married. He came west with John T. Beal in the late 1800s and settled in the Ranger Lake area north of Tatum. He worked for the XIT and drove cattle to Abilene with Beal. In his later years, he ran a pool hall in Lovington. Logan lived into his eighties.[11]

Dolph Lusk was a cowboy on the latter-day open range of present-day Lea County, c. 1894-1905. He cowboyed for the Hat Ranch, which at that time must have been the area's biggest employer. Apparently he prospered, as he founded, with seven others, the First National Bank of Lovington; and with three others built a drug store, a hardware store, a furniture store, and the Commercial Hotel, one of Lovington's landmarks, all in 1918. His wife, Georgia Witt, was Lea County School Superintendent (1925-1928) and elected to Congress (1946-1948). One of his sons, Gene, ran for governor of New Mexico in 1966.[12]

Thomas N. (Shorty) Miller was born in 1872 in Tennessee, came west with his mother, married in 1906, and died in 1949. He worked for the Matador Ranch and homesteaded in the Knowles community in Lea County in 1906.[13]

Bill Oden was an open range cowboy for Frank Divers in 1884 at the old TAX Ranch. He bought a one-sixth interest in that operation, then sold his interest back to Divers in 1893. Oden was apparently an innovative cowboy. He "got permission to tinker over" the windmills Divers had, the strokes of which were too short, the slats too close together, and overall were considered too slow. He sped up the mills by taking out every other blade and lengthening the stroke. Oden also replaced wooden water containers then in use on the plains with surface tanks. Oden, known as Bill Tax as often as he was called by his real name, wrote his remembrances in 1965.[14]

Tom Ogle was a Hat cowboy at some time during the period 1894-1905.[15]

Blaton Ramsey of Pecos, Texas, was wagon boss for the Hat Ranch, c. 1902.[16]

Ed Ramsey of Seminole, Texas, was range boss for the Hat about 1902.[17]

Stumpie Roundtree was a wagon boss for the JAL, advancing to foreman by 1912.[18]

Shorty _____, an ex-Jingle Bob cowhand whose surname has not survived in recorded history, was an elderly man who "stayed in a line camp near the west breaks of the plains." Shorty met his end when he froze to death during a storm in the 1890s and was buried out on the caprock (Mescalero Ridge escarpment).[19]

Tom Vest was a cowboy for the Hat during the period 1894-1905, although his exact years of tenure with that major open range outfit are not known.[20]

Charlie Walker was reportedly with Littlefield on trail drives to Kansas. About 1905 when present-day Lea County was still open range, he "ran big steers with John Tyson." He was also a wagon boss for the LFD. Walker's brother Walter was a cowboy as well.[21]

Walter Walker was known as "Big Spider or Tarantula because he was crippled with rheumatism or arthritis." Apparently the affliction did not hinder his working as a cowboy. He worked for the LFD, as did his brother Charlie.[22]

Slick Warren was a Hat cowboy at some time during the period 1894-1905, and he may also be the cowboy whose Christian name was Ben (Warren) who was with the Hat in 1902.[23]

Bud Wilkerson, according to one source, was one of the cowboys who had been with the LFD since trail driving days, "when they had helped Major Littlefield drive herds of longhorn cattle to the rail heads in Kansas." Another source has documented that Wilkerson was a wagon boss for the LFD, and still a third source states that while with the LFD he was allowed to accumulate several hundred head of cattle himself and later put down the HUT well where he had his own small operation. If a relationship existed between Bud and Dick Wilkerson, an old buffalo hunter who was at Monument Springs in 1879, no documentation to that effect has been found.[24]

An additional thirteen men are known to have worked as cowboys in Lea County while it was open range country: John House, Doc Sears, Bruce Conner, Dave Howell, George Urton, Tom York, Will McCombs, Max Tabner, Fate Biard, Charlie Abers (also known as Bill Nye), Bob Honley (also known as Rain-in-the-Face), John Cole, and Joe Champion. Nothing more about these men is known.[25]

Notes

Chapter 1

1 James Irving Fenton, "Tom Ross: Outlaw and Stockman" (Unpublished Masters Thesis, University of Texas at El Paso, 1979), p. 45.

2 As quoted in the *American Historical Review,* July 1936, and numerous other places. The direct quotation, in part, read: "the unsettled area [of the United States] has been so broken into by isolated bodies of settlement that there can hardly be said to be a frontier line." As has accurately been pointed out by Fred A. Shannon in "The Homestead Act and the Labor Surplus," in this same issue of *American Historical Review:*

> The Superintendent of the Census was very cautious in the phraseology of his statement, and Professor Turner, in his original essay, did not attempt to read more into the sentence than its literal meaning conveyed. But long repetition, without frequent reference to the original text, plays tricks with the memory. Within a few years students were being told that by 1890 the frontier was gone, next that by 1890 the West was filled up with settlers, and finally that by 1890 all the free land in the West had been homesteaded.

3 Fenton, "Tom Ross", p. 44.

4 *New Mexico Statistical Abstract* (Albuquerque: University of New Mexico, Bureau of Business and Economic Research, 1989), p. 176.

5 *13th Census of the United States. 1910. New Mexico.* Chaves County, Volume 2, 1-206; Eddy County, Vol. 4, 1-288.

6 *New Mexico Statistical Abstract,* p. 176.

7 Ibid.

8 Gil Hinshaw. *Lea, New Mexico's Last Frontier* (Hobbs: Hobbs Daily News-Sun, 1976), p. 74.

9 Ibid., p. 105.

10 Ibid., p. 108.

11 *The Gaines County Story: A History of Gaines County, Texas* (Seagraves, Texas: Pioneer Book Publishers, 1974), p. 2.

12 *Early Settlers of Terry: A History of Terry County, Texas* (Hereford, Texas: Pioneer Book Publishers, Inc., 1968), p. 11.

13 V. H. Whitlock, *Cowboy Life on the Llano Estacado* (Norman: University of Oklahoma Press, 1970), p. 227.

14 Hinshaw, *Lea, New Mexico's Last Frontier,* pp. 75-76.

15 Fenton, "Tom Ross," p. 47. Fenton also quotes from p. 195 of *The Gaines County Story:* "There were a lot of tough characters who plied the rustling trade across the border [from Texas into New Mexico]." The implication is clearly that the area was not without its marginal element. One of the tales repeated locally is that while the Highlonesome headquarters house was being constructed (from caliche rock), a man on the run rode by and asked that his wooden-handled revolver be hidden in the wide adobe and rock walls as they went up. Another story often repeated concerns three men who in

1912 robbed the Seminole, Texas, bank in neighboring Gaines County, and then fled back across the state line where one of their group was murdered by the other two and left on the San Simon range.

16 Ibid., pp. 3, 4, 35, 189; S. R. Simpson, *Llano Estacado: or the Plains of West Texas* (San Antonio: The Naylor Company 1957), pp. 11-13.

17 Sarah Shelton to C. J. Brooks, interview, January 17, 1991. This information about Gravy Field was first discovered in unpublished notes made by Sylvia Benge Mahoney when she interviewed Bobby and Sarah Field, November 1, 1980. Notes are located in the archives of the Lea County Cowboy Hall of Fame and Western Heritage Center, Hobbs, New Mexico.

18 Bob Beverly, *Hobo of the Rangeland: 100 Laughs for 100 Cents,* n.d., pp. 22-58.

19 *Then and Now,* Volume I, p. 313.

20 Ibid., p. 128.

21 Price, *Open Range Ranching,* p. 56.

1 Cordelia Sloan Duke and Joe B. Frantz, *6,000 Miles of Fence* (Austin: University of Texas Press, 1961), p. 209.

2 As quoted in John C. Dawson, Sr., *High Plains Yesterdays: From XIT Days Through Drouth and Depression* (Austin: Eakin Press, 1985), p. 5.

3 Clifford P. Westermeier, *Trailing the Cowboy: His Life and Lore as Told by Frontier Journalists* (Caldwell, Idaho: Caxton Printers, 1955), p. 18.

4 David Brion Davis, "Ten Gallon Hero," *American Quarterly* (Summer, 1954), pp. 112-14.

5 Hinshaw, *Lea, New Mexico's Last Frontier,* p. 74.

6 In addition to the seventeen Texans, two each were from Missouri and Georgia, and one each were from Indian Territory, Georgia, Kansas, Arkansas, South Carolina, Tennessee, Alabama, Mississippi, and Louisiana. Far removed from any Southern influence were the two cowboys from Germany and one from New York.

7 Haley, *Men of Fiber,* p. 33.

8 *Then and Now,* Volume I, pp. 110-17.

9 Lugene Howry to C. J. Brooks, interview, January 3, 1990.

10 Lura Benson to C. J. Brooks, interview, January 17, 1990.

11 Fenton, "Tom Ross," p. 2.

12 Biographical information about Alfred Green Rushing was gathered from his children still living in 1982 on the occasion of Green's induction into the Lea County Cowboy Hall of Fame and Western Heritage Center.

13 As quoted in William W. Savage, Jr., editor, *Cowboy Life: Reconstructing an American Myth* (Norman: University of Oklahoma Press, 1975), p. 77.

14 Joe B. Frantz and Julian Ernest Choate, Jr., *The American Cowboy: The Myth and the Reality* (Norman: University of Oklahoma Press, 1955), p. 97: "He may have been merely a unique occupational type who was concerned with 'cow work'. . . ."

15 Ibid., pp. 8-9.

16 *Then and Now,* Volume I, p. 22-23.

17 Cleo Heidel Fuchs to C. J. Brooks, interview, January 3, 1990.

18 Duke and Frantz, *6,000 Miles of Fence,* pp. 209, 214, 216. The authors state that the "most likely post-cowboy career for an XIT hand [other than ranching] was some sort of peace officer." Ten cowboys in this study went on to become full-time ranchers (defined here as someone operating at least a 10-section ranch where outside employment was not necessary for subsistence). Six cowboys in this study (18 percent) entered the field of law enforcement.

19 Biographical information about Bob Beverly was gathered over a period of several weeks from his son, Walter Beverly, occasioned by the elder Beverly's induction into the Lea County Cowboy Hall of Fame and Western Heritage Center in 1985. Notes are in the archives of that Center.

20 *Then and Now,* Volume I, p. 313.

21 Ibid., pp. 110-17.

22 Ibid., pp. 9-11.

23 Anemone Love Binkley to C. J. Brooks, interview, January 3, 1990.

24 Notes in the archives of New Mexico Junior College, Pannell Library, Oral History Collection, and in the archives of the Lea County Cowboy Hall of Fame and Western Heritage Center.

25 The post-cowboy occupations of Lea Countians are not at great variance from pre-ranching occupations of the cattlemen studied by Atherton [Lewis Atherton, *The Cattle Kings* (Bloomington: Indiana University Press, 1967), p. 3]: mining, law enforcement, freighting, trail driving, stage driving, steamboat piloting, railroaders, blacksmiths, painters, plumbers, army men, politicians, bankers, teachers, hotelkeepers.

26 From J. Frank Dobie's *A Vaquero of the Brush Country,* as quoted in John Hendrix, *If I Can Do It Horseback: A Cow-Country Sketchbook* (Austin: University of Texas Press, 1964), p. 6.

27 *13th Census of the United States. 1910, New Mexico, Chaves County,* Volume 2, 1-206; Eddy County, Volume 4, 1-288. Indeed, even when comparing the old open range cowboys of Lea County with the younger generation of men who, in 1910, still claimed to be cowboys, differences are identifiable. For example, the thirty-two old open range cowboys identified here were all married, and thirty-one had children. On the average, the men in the younger group were twenty-one years old, and only three of them were married.

28 Savage, *Cowboy Life,* p. 7

29 *13th Census of the United States.* One cowboy from among those in the primary study group cited "day laborer" as his trade or profession, and "odd jobs" as the "general nature of industry." Other livestock-related occupations enumerated from among the general population of Lea County and their frequency were: herder/sheep, thirty-six; stockman/ranch, sixteen; stock farmer/cattle,

thirteen; stockman/cattle, ten; sheepman/ranch, nine; stockman/ sheep, seven; stockman/horses, six; foreman/ranch, five; horsetrader, four; stock farmer/cattle ranch, three; and manager/ sheep ranch, one. Paradoxically, one man reported that his occupation was a farmer and the place he did his farming was a ranch. Statistics, reasonably, are victims of nomenclature.

30 Among the thirty-two cowboys studied, two raised sheep—one on an occasional basis as market trends demanded and the other as a major sheep rancher who raised some cattle on the side.

31 Anemone Love Binkley, interview.

32 Bill Oden, *Early Days on the Texas-New Mexico Plains* (J. Evetts Haley, editor, Canyon, Texas: Palo Duro Press, 1965), p. 44.

33 Duke and Frantz, *6,000 Miles of Fence,* p. 209.

34 *Then and Now,* Volume I, p. 533. Wright attended Add-Ran, the forerunner of Texas Christian University.

35 Ibid., p. 394.

36 According to Don Hedgpeth, *The Texas Breed: A Cowboy Anthology* (Flagstaff: Northland Press, 1978), p. 2, Joseph McCoy was uncomplimentary to cowboys, saying they had "little, if any, taste for reading." James D. Shinkle, *Fifty Years of Roswell History, 1867-1917,* (Roswell, New Mexico: Hall-Poorbaugh Press, 1964), p. 55, claimed of the old open range cowboys, "Many . . . could neither read nor write their names. . . ." Another source concurs: "The Texas herder, provided he can read at all, takes along a stray copy of the *Police Gazette* or a Beadle novel," Westermeier, *Trailing the Cowboy,* p. 27. The following balanced, and more contemporary, evaluation (in a publication edited by Charles F. Lummis and Charles Amadon Moody) claims: "Though the cowboy is not a college graduate he is by [no] means an ignoramus; usually he is . . . fairly well read,

taking the same active interest in current topics and politics" as others. From J. Albert Mallory, "The Cowboy of Today," *Out West: A Magazine of the Old Pacific and the New* (January-June, 1908), p. 224.

37 Anemone Love Binkley, interview.

38 Glen Adams to C. J. Brooks, interviews, 1987-1989.

39 J. B. Tidwell to C. J. Brooks, interview, October 25, 1983.

40 Savage, *Cowboy Life,* p. 5.

41 Dobie, *A Vaquero of the Brush Country,* p. 1.

42 *13th Census of the United States.*

43 Clifford P. Westermeier, "The Cowboy and Sex" in *The Cowboy: Six-Shooters, Songs, and Sex* (Norman: University of Oklahoma Press, 1976), p. 86.

44 Savage, *Cowboy Life,* p. 6.

45 Ibid., p. 41.

46 James H. Cook, *Fifty Years on the Frontier: as Cowboy, Hunter, Guide, Scout, and Ranchman* (Norman: University of Oklahoma Press, [1923], 1963), p. xiii.

47 For some of the cowboys who left home at a very young age, the possibility of becoming lost in a crowd of anonymous cowboys may have been a barrier between them and irate parents or even lawmen.

48 This same cowboy, according to two sources, "burned out" several nesters, the only documented local case this writer has discovered of problems between open range ranchers (or cowboys)

and homesteaders. Local legend describes Lewis as a "scary character" who often ranted about being "from Jerusalem." (Glen Adams, interviews; Lura Benson interview).

49 *Then and Now,* Volume I, p. 110.

50 For a detailed discussion of this man, refer to Fenton, "Tom Ross," cited earlier.

51 *A Man Called Jim,* p. 153.

52 Lura Benson, interview.

53 Precise details on causes of death are not included in this study.

54 Glen Adams, interviews; Lura Benson, interview.

55 Ball, Eve, "Henry Record was Muy Hombre," *Frontier Times,* February-March, 1976, p. 64; information about Record's philanthropy can be found in numerous accounts of his life, several of which are on file at the Lea County Cowboy Hall of Fame and Western Heritage Center, Hobbs, New Mexico, gathered on the occasion of his induction into the Hall in 1978.

56 Beverly and Price from the primary study group both wrote their recollections, cited elsewhere. In addition, Beverly was asked to write his recollections for Cordelia Duke, the XIT ranch manager's wife (see Duke and Frantz, *6,000 Miles of Fence*). Bill Oden from among the secondary group (Appendix B) also wrote his memoirs, cited earlier.

57 Jerome O. Steffen, *Comparative Frontiers: A Proposal for Studying the American West* (Norman: University of Oklahoma Press, 1980), p. 55.

58 *The Historical Encyclopedia of New Mexico,* p. 122.

59 Clifford Gray to C. J. Brooks, interview, January 16, 1990.

60 *13th Census of the United States.* "Neighboring" in the vernacular, is the act of assisting one another with ranch work, such as branding, without compensation.

1 May Price Mosley, *Little Texas Beginnings in Southeastern New Mexico* (Roswell, New Mexico: Hall-Poorbaugh Press, 1973), pp. 95-122.

2 Binkley, *A Man Called Jim,* p. 166.

3 Brief biographies of each of the thirty-two cowboys in the primary study group may be found in Appendix A.

4 Binkley, *A Man Called Jim,* p. 126.

5 Mallory, *Out West,* p. 222-23.

6 William Curry Holden, *Alkali Trails: Or Social and Economic Movements of the Texas Frontier 1846-1900* (Dallas: The Southwest Press), pp. 176-85.

7 *Then and Now,* Volume I, p. 10.

8 Laverne Burk Shaw to C. J. Brooks, interview, January 3, 1990.

9 Ray Allen Billington, *The Westward Movement in the United States* (Princeton, New Jersey: D. Van Nostrand Co., Inc., 1959), p. 88.

10 The idea of continuity in the establishment of institutions as frontiers are settled has been developed by historian Jerome O. Steffen and Earl Pomeroy before him.

11 Billington, *The Westward Movement,* p. 88.

12 F. Logan Beal to C. J. Brooks, interview, January 17, 1990.

13 Price, *Open Range Ranching on the South Plains in the 1890s,* p. 67. Other information about Eidson has been gleaned from miscellaneous local newspaper reports, such as a social note about a bridge party at the Eidson home, as well as information gathered on the

occasion of Eidson's induction into the Lea County Cowboy Hall of Fame and Western Heritage Center in 1987.

14 Larry McMurtry, "Take My Saddle from the Wall," *Harpers,* (September, 1968), p. 45, as quoted by Clifford P. Westermeier, "The Cowboy and Sex," in *The Cowboy: Six-Shooters, Songs, and Sex* (Norman: University of Oklahoma Press, 1976).

15 David Brion Davis, "Ten Gallon Hero," p. 117.

16 Ibid.

17 See biographical data on each cowboy, included in Appendix A.

18 *13th Census of the United States.* The statistics presented for these latter-day cowboys represent only the communities of Lovington and Monument due to the difficulty in isolating those individuals who actually lived within the boundaries of present-day Lea County. These cowboys differed in other respects from the former open range cowboys under study. Their average age at the 1910 census was 21.6, with a total of fourteen being in their teens. Without the inclusion of two older-than-average cowboys (one thirty-two and one forty-six, married, with two children), the average age was 20.5.

19 Price's recollections have been published under the title *Open Range Ranching on the South Plains in the 1890s,* cited earlier, one of the more credible local histories. See particularly pp. 18, 19, 31, and 66.

20 *The Knowles News Plains Special,* 1910.

21 Information about Robert Florence Love and James Benjamin Love may be found in numerous sources, including *Then and Now,* Volume I, pp. 9-13 and 191-92. Additional data was obtained in an interview with Anemone Love Binkley, January 3, 1990, and in *A Man Called Jim.*

22 Ibid.

23 Donna Medlin to C. J. Brooks, interview, October 1988. Medlin, Price's granddaughter, provided biographical data on the occasion of his induction into the Lea County Cowboy Hall of Fame and Western Heritage Center, 1988. Notes in the archives of that Center.

24 *The Knowles News Plains Special,* 1910. With respect to Allen Heard, he was the son of a sheep rancher "so poor he couldn't afford to purchase a can of sardines," an incident that so piqued Heard that he set out on his own at fifteen, and eventually became one of the major landholders and community builders in Lea County.

25 *13th Census. 1910. New Mexico.* By way of illustrating the deficiencies of these early census reports, only eight individuals cited among *all* the cowboys in this book were even enumerated on the census, and those were individuals who were living in established communities, making them accessible to the census enumerators. Seven were from the primary study group and one was from the secondary group (Appendix B). Aside from the Love brothers and Heard, the other former cowboys (though also involved in banking and community service) gave their occupations as either stockman or cattleman rather than cowboy. One, J. D. Hart, who helped establish the first bank in Lovington and was a major rancher, was listed as a "squatter" by the census enumerator.

26 Robert N. Bellah, et al. *Habits of the Heart: Individualism and Commitment in American Life* (Berkeley: University of California Press, 1985), p. 153. Bellah said:

[W]e can speak of a real community as a 'community of memory,' one that does not forget its past. In order not to forget that past, a community is involved in retelling its story, its constitutive narrative, and in so doing, it offers examples of the men and women who have embodied and exemplified the meaning of the community.

27 Weigle and White, *The Lore of New Mexico,* p. 235.

28 Mosley, *Little Texas Beginnings,* p. 95.

29 *Then and Now: Lea County Families,* Volume II. (Lovington, New Mexico: Lea County Genealogical Society, 1984), p. 26.

30 Bob Beverly, "That Flaxey Horse," *The Cattleman* (November 1952), p. 100.

31 Robert G. Athearn, *The Mythic West in Twentieth Century America* (Lawrence: University of Kansas Press, 1986) p. 29.

32 Information about the XIT reunions, commencing in 1936, is found in many places, including John C. Dawson, Jr.'s *High Plains Yesterdays: From XIT Days Through Drouth and Depression* (Austin: Eakin Press, 1985). Pertinent to this study is a small booklet published at Dalhart, Texas, in 1939 entitled *Cowhands of the XIT,* in which seven men who later made Lea County their home are listed: Dory Burks [sic], Bob Beverly, Lewis Derrick, H. Fields [sic], Pat McClure, Jim Anderson, and S. R. Cooper. Interestingly (and in support of the thesis that working as a cowboy was a rather insignificant part of these men's history) some descendants never mentioned these men's XIT experiences when writing about the men. Perhaps the cowboys themselves never stressed this aspect of their history.

33 *Then and Now,* Volume II, p. 26. Two of the three founders of the Open Range Cowboys Association in Lea County were cowboys under study here: Bob Beverly and Jim Love; and one, Henry Record, was its first president.

34 Jimmy M. Skaggs. *The Cattle-Trailing Industry: Between Supply and Demand, 1866-1890* (Lawrence: The University Press of Kansas, 1973), p. 120. Skaggs suggests that by 1889 the "cattle trails— blocked by law—were a fading memory."

35 Frantz and Choate, *The American Cowboy,* p. 67, write, "By 1892, the story of the frontier ranch and its cowboys had already been lived, and many cowboys were getting ready to reminisce in print and at cowboy reunions."

36 References to the clannishness of cowboys are many, among which are excerpts from "The Cowboy's Life" (*El anunciador de Trinidad,* (Trinidad, Colorado, December 1, 1887), as quoted in Westermeier, *Trailing the Cowboy,* p. 29, and Alfred Henry Lewis, *Wolfville Nights,* 1902, as cited in Savage, *Cowboy Life,* p. 158.

37 Fenton, "Tom Ross", p. 70. The author states: "The cattle fraternity was small . . . [and] to be . . . open or straight-forward about . . . [one's] personal life was not the nature of the old-time cowman whom [Ross] so well exemplified." This cliché about cowboys has been repeated in many sources, such as *The Cowboys,* part of a series about the West written by William H. Forbis and published by Time-Life Books (New York: Time, Inc., 1973), p. 20.

38 William H. Forbis, *The Cowboys* (*The Old West Series*), (New York: Time, Inc., 1973), p. 30.

39 Westermeier, *Trailing the Cowboy,* p. 250, quoting from the *Texas Live Stock Journal* (Ft. Worth, Texas, January 21, 1888), p. 15.

40 Atherton, *The Cattle Kings,* p. 129.

41 Davis, "Ten Gallon Hero," p. 121.

42 Atherton, *The Cattle Kings,* p. 129.

43 Ibid., p. 131.

44 Margaret Walter McGuffin to C. J. Brooks, interview, January 3, 1990.

45 James Elmer Rowan, "Agricultural Land Utilization in the Llano Estacado of Eastern New Mexico and Western Texas" (Unpublished Doctoral Dissertation, University of Nebraska, 1960), p. 95.

46 Bellah, *Habits of the Heart,* p. 219.

47 Holden, *Alkali Trails,* p. 175.

48 George Thorp to C. J. Brooks, interview, January 3, 1990. Thorp, son of Creed Thorp, was expressing his father's feelings about the "hereafter".

49 Fenton, "Tom Ross", pp. 76-77.

50 Earl Pomeroy, "Toward a Reorientation of Western History: Continuity and Environment," *Mississippi Valley Historical Review* (June 1954-March 1955), pp. 581-82.

51 D. W. Meinig, *Imperial Texas: An Interpretive Essay in Cultural Geography* (Austin: University of Texas Press, 1969), p. 82.

52 The first documented use of the term "Little Texas" is found in May Price Mosley's book, *Little Texas Beginnings in Southeastern New Mexico,* cited earlier. Meinig and others have since used the term.

53 Pomeroy, "Toward a Reorientation of Western History," pp. 596-97.

54 Athearn, *The Mythic West in Twentieth Century America,* p. 29. In Gregory M. Tobin's *The Making of a History: Walter Prescott Webb and The Great Plains* (Austin: University of Texas Press, 1976), p. 123, we see the best spokesmen of the alternative view represented,

wherein it is written that Edward Everett Dale became convinced that "Webb was correct in his contention that in the broader cultural sense the West was not simply an extension of the East but something distinct and unique." Webb does concede, however, that the small Texas plains towns did come about "with most of the structural requirements of organized society already in place."

55 William W. Savage, Jr., *The Cowboy Hero: His Image in American History and Culture* (Norman: University of Oklahoma Press, 1979), p. 14. Savage asked: "Were western communities structured to reward that sort of common experience?"

1 Savage, *The Cowboy Hero,* p. 3.

2 Hendrix, *If I Can Do It Horseback.* In this instance, the title is more significant than the contents.

3 Ibid., p. 3.

4 From *Prose and Poetry of the Live Stock Industry of the United States,* as quoted in Savage, *Cowboy Life,* p. 172.

5 Walt Wiggins, *New Mexico Cockleburs and Cow Chips* (Roswell, New Mexico: Western Heritage Press, 1975), pp. 72-73.

6 Hedgpeth, *The Texas Breed,* pp. 118-19.

7 Skaggs, *Cattle-Trailing,* p. 52. One such cowboy, Pryor by name, reportedly told his employer in 1871, "You can take your plow and go to hell," after which he "set out to find work as a drover."

8 Billington, *The Westward Movement,* p. 82.

9 *Then and Now,* Volume I, p. 259.

10 Price, *Open Range Ranching on the South Plains in the 1890s,* p. 68.

11 Savage, *Cowboy Life,* p. 6. It should be emphasized that the sample of open range cowboys who came to Lea County to make their homes may be neither statistically significant nor representative. Savage has written, "The cowboy was a wage earner, not a capitalist, and only occasionally did he—or could he—rise above that economic level to acquire land or cattle of his own." But apparently the industry itself believed the transition from cowboy to cowman was possible for this quote was taken from *Prose and Poetry of the Live Stock Industry of the United States,* and quoted by Savage in *Cowboy*

Life, p. 175: "[M]any [cowboys] . . . saved their wages, and successfully became range-stockmen on their own account in later years." And Atherton has documented the fact that many of the Texas cattle kings had themselves been cowboys at first (*The Cattle Kings,* p. 106).

12 Price, *Open Range Ranching,* p. 48.

13 James M. Marshall, *Land Fever: Dispossession and Frontier Myth* (Lexington: University Press of Kentucky, 1986), p. 109.

14 Rowan, "Agricultural Land Utilization in the Llano Estacado," p. 110.

15 Laverne Burk Shaw to C. J. Brooks, interview, January 3, 1990.

16 This paradox and other problems associated with the Homestead Act of 1862 led Billington (*The Westward Movement,* p. 83) to say that the Act did not help populate the West as intended and that "[S]even or eight pioneers had to pay heavily for every one receiving a farm as a gift from the government." The Lea County cowboys, however, appear to have made the best of this public land policy.

17 George A. Wallis, *Cattle Kings of the Staked Plains* (Denver: Sage Books, 1964), p. 154.

18 J. Evetts Haley, *Charles Goodnight: Cowman and Plainsman* (Norman: University of Oklahoma Press, 1949), p. 388.

19 *13th Census of the United States.*

20 Today it requires about ten sections of land to make a minimal living ranching fulltime in Lea County (there are 640 acres per section), so ten sections is used in this book as the line of demarcation between those who could be termed ranchers and those who were more nearly stock farmers.

21 Henry Record's sizeable estate has been discussed elsewhere in this study. Millard Eidson, V. M. Chambers, and Allen C. Heard were also reportedly wealthy men by any standard.

22 Athearn, *The Mythic West in Twentieth Century America,* p. 27. Athearn further suggests a great disparity between cowboys and responsible stock raisers:

> A young man interested in stock raising had a choice: he could become a typical cowboy nuisance, wear queer clothes, shoot off pistols and strange oaths to frighten tenderfeet, or he ... [could] become a real ranchman. The emphasis was on *real,* meaning one who recognized churches, schools, broadcloth suits, and business methods as a more normal way of life.

There is no indication that any such comically divergent choices played a role in the lives of the cowboys under study here. On the contrary, Savage was probably correct when he surmised that cowboys were dull (*Cowboy Life,* p. 7). A more contemporary piece called "The Cowboy of Today" by J. Albert Mallory appeared in Charles F. Lummis' magazine *Out West,* pp. 222-23. Mallory contended that cowboys differed "very little from the average American working youth...;" further, "The days of the modern cowboy ... are as full of hard and monotonous work as those of an eastern farm hand, and there is very little difference in the intellectual or social status of the two."

1 As quoted from Bernard DeVoto in Rita Parks, *The Western Hero in Film and Television: Mass Media Mythology* (Ann Arbor, Michigan: UMI Research Press, 1982), p. 17.

2 William W. Savage, Jr., in his essay entitled "The Cowboy Myth," places cowboys in that niche, a seemingly accurate pegging [*The Cowboy: Six Shooters, Songs, and Sex,* Charles Harris and Buck Rainey, editors (Norman: University of Oklahoma Press, 1976), p. 154].

3 David Dary., *Cowboy Culture: A Saga of Five Centuries* (New York: Avon, 1981), p. 332.

4 *Then and Now,* Volume I, p. 394.

5 Vicki Pierarski, "Cowboys, Cattlemen, and the Cattle Industry," in *The Frontier Experience: A Reader's Guide to the Life and Literature of the American West,* edited by Jon Tuska and Vicki Pierarski (Jefferson, North Carolina: McFarland and Company, 1984), p. 128.

6 Rita Parks, *The Western Hero in Film and Television,* pp. 1-2.

7 Westermeier, *Trailing the Cowboy,* p. 22.

8 Frantz and Choate, *The American Cowboy,* p. 82.

9 Thomas L. Hartshorne, *The Distorted Image: Changing Conceptions of the American Character Since Turner* (Cleveland: The Press of Case Western Reserve University, 1968), p. 3.

10 Ibid., p. 189.

11 Duke and Frantz, *6,000 Miles of Fence,* p. ix. (Men who formerly cowboyed for the XIT were no strangers to present Lea County, for the northeast corner of Lea joined the southwest corner of the XIT. Hinshaw, *Lea, New Mexico's Last Frontier,* p. 75.)

12 Written by Dobie in his foreword to James H. Cook's *Fifty Years on the Frontier: as Cowboy, Hunter, Guide, Scout, and Ranchman* (Norman: University of Oklahoma Press, 1923), p. viii.

13 Pierarski, "Cowboys, Cattlemen, and the Cattle Industry," p.140.

14 J. Evetts Haley lauded Bob Beverly in his *Men of Fiber* (El Paso: Carl Hertzog, 1963), pp. 31-39. Bob Beverly was often quoted by Haley and even J. Frank Dobie. Beverly wrote a small book called *Hobo of the Rangeland,* and he wrote stories for *The Cattleman* and *New Mexico Stockman* over a period of years, c. 1930s-1950s. Beverly (and perhaps even Siringo and others) spun yarns because he was *paid* to do so.

15 Dobie, *A Vaquero of the Brush Country,* p. 105.

16 Savage, "The Cowboy Myth," in *The Cowboy,* p. 156.

17 Jerome O. Steffen, "Insular v. Cosmopolitan Frontiers: A Proposal for the Comparative Study of American Frontiers," *The American West: New Perspectives, New Dimensions,* edited by Jerome O. Steffen (Norman: University of Oklahoma Press, 1979), p. 116.

18 Richard W. Etulain, "Western Fiction and History," *The American West: New Perspectives, New Dimensions,* p. 171.

19 Florid prose of the nineteenth and early twentieth centuries could have contributed unwittingly to the romanticizing of cowboys and Western history in general. For example, in 1910 in Lea County

the readership of the *Knowles News* was introduced to a new deputy in town with the following sketch:

> Yea, verily, and in very sooth, doth a man have to be born with a desire and a liking for the task of putting himself up as a living target for vicious, bloodthirsty transgressors of the law, to hurl leaden missiles of deadly defiance at (as quoted by Hinshaw, Lea, *New Mexico's Last Frontier*, p. 118.)

The prose was not only florid, but flawed. Research has shown that there were few transgressors and they could hardly be termed either vicious or blood-thirsty. This example of mythologizing the role of a deputy sheriff is analogous to mythologizing cowboys.

20 Laverne Burk Shaw, interview.

21 Jim McCauley wrote in *A Stove-up Cowboy's Story,* "When you grow up to anything 'tis hard to quit and have to try something else. . . ," as quoted in Hedgpeth, *The Texas Breed,* p. 37.

22 Mallory, "The Cowboy of Today," *Out West,* p. 224.

23 Skaggs, *Cattle-Trailing,* p. 123.

24 Atherton, *The Cattle Kings,* p. 107.

25 The Permian Basin accounts for more than 20 percent of the total U. S. oil and gas production, as cited by Gus Clemens, *Legacy: The Story of the Permian Basin Region of West Texas and Southeast New Mexico* (San Antonio: Mulberry Avenue Books, 1983), p. 9. Lea County, the area under study here, is a part of the Permian Basin, and in the past has been the largest oil producing county in the United States. Those early-day open range cowboys who had the foresight to retain the mineral rights to the acreage they home-steaded or acquired otherwise have become immensely wealthy

from oil and gas production. In fact, it is a commonly held belief that most of the large landholders would not have survived by just ranching alone, an irony in view of their legendary distaste for the "oilpatch." All the land is good for, one old rancher has been quoted as saying, is "collecting damages from oil men." [Quotation attributed to W. D. "Jiggs" Dinwiddie, a modern-day rancher at Jal, New Mexico, by Bert Madera, another Jal rancher, in a conversation with C. J. Brooks, c. April 1988.]

26 Ball, "Henry Record was Muy Hombre," p. 17.

27 Price, *Open Range Ranching,* p. 3. Price, in his rosy recollection of the early days on the Llano Estacado admits, "In a way it was sport. Sport with a meaning," by which he points out that an outsider might certainly view ranch work differently than one engaged in it on a daily basis.

28 Ruth Kessler Rice, *Letters from New Mexico 1899-1904* (Albuquerque, New Mexico: Adobe Press, 1981), pp. 8-9.

29 Ibid., p. 49.

30 Parks, *The Western Hero in Film and Television,* pp. 1-2.

31 Athearn, *The Mythic West in Twentieth Century America,* p. 6.

32 Mallory, "The Cowboy of Today," *Out West,* p. 224.

33 Parks, *The Western Hero in Film and Television,* p. 46.

34 Ibid.

Appendix A

1 *Then and Now,* Volume I, pp. 356 and 391; *Cowhands of the XIT;* Lorena Easley to C. J. Brooks, interview, December 20, 1990; *The Historical Encyclopedia of New Mexico* (Albuquerque: New Mexico Historical Association, 1945), p. 1344.

2 F. Logan Beal to C. J. Brooks, interview, January 17, 1990; Graydon Dean, Jr. to C. J. Brooks, letter, December 13, 1989.

3 Graydon Dean, Jr. to C. J. Brooks, letter, December 13, 1989; F. Logan Beal, "The Beal Family of Ranger Lake," in *Then and Now– Lea County Families,* Volume I, Lea County Genealogical Society, Lovington, New Mexico, 1979, pp. 234-35. F. Logan Beal to C. J. Brooks, interview, January 17, 1990.

4 Haley, *Men of Fiber,* p. 33; Bob Beverly, *Hobo of the Rangeland: 100 Laughs for 100 Cents,* n.d., p. 54; Hinshaw, *Lea, New Mexico's Last Frontier,* p. 121; Duke and Frantz, *6,000 Miles of Fence,* pp. 46-47, 84, 91-92, 199; *Cowhands of the XIT; The Historical Encyclopedia of New Mexico,* p. 1221.

5 *Then and Now,* Volume I, p. 313.

6 Ibid., pp. 174-76; *Then and Now,* Volume II, p. 89; Hinshaw, *Lea, New Mexico's Last Frontier,* p. 121; Ira Breckon to C. J. Brooks, interview, August 17, 1990.

7 *Then and Now,* Volume II, p. 91; *Odessa American,* November 2, 1958; *Cowhands of the XIT;* Laverne Burk Shaw to C. J. Brooks, interview, January 3, 1990.

8 *Then and Now,* Volume I, p. 394.

9 *Then and Now,* Volume I, pp. 256-61; *Cowhands of the XIT.*

10 *Then and Now,* Volume I, pp. 110-17.

11 *Then and Now,* Volume II, p. 468; *Cowhands of the XIT; Lovington Leader,* June, 1952; Pearl Dunlap to C. J. Brooks, interview, January 11, 1991.

12 Price, *Open Range Ranching on the South Plains in the 1890s,* p. 67; *The Gaines County Story,* p. 45.

13 Sarah Shelton to C. J. Brooks, interview, January 17, 1991. This interview corroborated information from unpublished notes about Gravy Field made by Sylvia Benge Mahoney when she interviewed Bobby and Sarah Field (now Sarah Shelton), November 1, 1980. These notes are located in the archives of the Lea County Cowboy Hall of Fame and Western Heritage Center, Hobbs, New Mexico. One other brief reference to Field appeared in an interview with Jim Love, another cowboy with the XIT, in the *Lovington Press,* October 9, 1958; *Cowhands of the XIT.*

14 *Then and Now,* Volume I, pp. 22-23.

15 Price, *Open Range Ranching,* p. 49; *Then and Now,* Volume I, p. 128.

16 Price, *Open Range Ranching,* p. 56.

17 Cleo Heidel Fuchs to C. J. Brooks, interview, January 3, 1990; *Then and Now,* Volume I, p. 245.

18 *Then and Now,* Volume II, pp. 222-23.

19 Lugene Howry to C. J. Brooks, interview, January 3, 1990; *Then and Now,* Volume II, p. 118; Michelle Manis, *The Beasley Connection,* Volume I, 1984, pp. 403, 421-22; Clemens, *Legacy,* pp. 110-11. The Lynch connection to the origin of the JAL brand has been reported in numerous sources.

20 Glen Adams to C. J. Brooks, interviews, 1987-1989; Lura Benson to C. J. Brooks, interview, January 17, 1990; unpublished notes from the archives of the Lea County Cowboy Hall of Fame and Western Heritage Center.

21 Anemone Love Binkley to C. J. Brooks, interview, January 3, 1990; *Then and Now*, Volume I, pp. 191-92; Binkley, *A Man Called Jim;* this book by Love's daughter is primarily about Jim B. Love's life.

22 *Then and Now*, Volume I, pp. 9-11; Anemone Love Binkley to C. J. Brooks, interview, January 3, 1990.

23 Faye McClure Kizer to C. J. Brooks, interview, December 19, 1990; *Then and Now*, Volume I, p. 346; *Cowhands of the XIT*; *The Historical Encyclopedia of New Mexico*, p. 1396.

24 Price, *Open Range Ranching*, pp. 18, 19, 31, 66.

25 Hinshaw, *Lea, New Mexico's Last Frontier*, p.111; Bob Beverly, "The Old Y Crossing," *The Cattleman*, February 1953, p. 125; Eve Ball, "Henry Record was Muy Hombre," *Frontier Times*, February-March 1976, pp. 62-64.

26 Fenton, "Tom Ross," pp. 3, 4, 35, 189; S. R. Simpson, *Llano Estacado: Or the Plains of West Texas* (San Antonio: The Naylor Company, 1957), pp. 11-13.

27 Hinshaw, *Lea, New Mexico's Last Frontier*, p. 94; *Then and Now*, Volume I, p. 14.

28 George Thorp to C. J. Brooks, interview, January 3, 1990; *Then and Now*, Volume II, p. 145; Gladys Thorp to C. J. Brooks, interview, January 17, 1990.

29 Margaret Walter McGuffin to C. J. Brooks, interview, January 3, 1990.

30 Clarabel Weir Tanner and Bert Ellen Weir Camp to Mettie Jordan, correspondence, October 1989, located in archives of Lea County Cowboy Hall of Fame and Western Heritage Center; Bob Beverly, "That Flaxey Horse," pp. 97-98.

31 *Then and Now*, Volume I, pp. 135-36; Price, *Open Range Ranching*, p. 56.

32 *Then and Now*, Volume I, pp. 533-34; personal family history (this cowboy was the author's husband's maternal grandfather).

Appendix B

1 Whitlock, *Cowboy Life on the Llano Estacado,* p. 136; *Then and Now,* Volume II, p. 487; Price, *Open Range Ranching,* pp. 50, 59.

2 Binkley, *A Man Called Jim,* pp. 125-26.

3 Price, *Open Range Ranching,* p. 58; Bob Beverly, "No Life for a Tenderfoot," *The Cattleman,* June 1950, p. 40.

4 Binkley, *A Man Called Jim,* p. 124.

5 Hinshaw, *Lea, New Mexico's Last Frontier,* p. 111.

6 *Then and Now,* Volume II, p. 180.

7 Whitlock, *Cowboy Life on the Llano Estacado,* p. 136; Hinshaw, *Lea, New Mexico's Last Frontier,* pp. 68, 80; Bill Zimmerman to C. J. Brooks, interview, April 25, 1990.

8 Binkley, *A Man Called Jim,* p. 134.

9 Ibid.

10 *Then and Now,* Volume II, p. 177-79; Hinshaw, *Lea, New Mexico's Last Frontier,* p. 121.

11 F. Logan Beal, interview, January 17, 1990; Graydon Dean, Jr., letter, December 13, 1989.

12 *Then and Now,* Volume I, pp. 301, 488; Hinshaw, *Lea, New Mexico's Last Frontier,* p. 94; *Then and Now,* Volume II, p. 20.

13 *Then and Now,* Volume II, p. 358.

14 Clemens, *Legacy,* pp. 128-29; Bill Oden, *Early Days on the Texas-New Mexico Plains,* p. 5.

15 Hinshaw, *Lea, New Mexico's Last Frontier,* p. 94.

16 Binkley, *A Man Called Jim,* p. 134.

17 Ibid.

18 Hinshaw, *Lea, New Mexico's Last Frontier,* p. 121; *Then and Now,* Volume II, pp. 179, 220.

19 Whitlock, *Cowboy Life on the Llano Estacado,* p. 75.

20 Hinshaw, *Lea, New Mexico's Last Frontier,* p. 94.

21 *Then and Now,* Volume I, p. 441; Hinshaw, *Lea, New Mexico's Last Frontier,* p. 121; Whitlock, *Cowboy Life on the Llano Estacado,* p. 136.

22 Whitlock, *Cowboy Life on the Llano Estacado,* p. 136.

23 Binkley, *A Man Called Jim,* p. 134.

24 Hinshaw, *Lea, New Mexico's Last Frontier,* p. 121; Whitlock, *Cowboy Life on the Llano Estacado,* p. 136; Price, *Open Range Ranching,* p. 48.

25 Whitlock, *Cowboy Life on the Llano Estacado,* p. 136. None of the cowboys in Appendix B were charter members of the Open Range Cowboys Association in Lea County. Perhaps by the 1930s when the organization was formed, these men had passed away or moved away (or perhaps they were disinterested in the group). Binkley, *A Man Called Jim,* p. 167, cites the following individuals as the first members of the Open Range Cowboys Association (with the comment, "Many of those people did not own ranches, or even a horse, at the time."): Dow Wood, Bob Beverly, Will Gray, M. G. Cottrell, J. B. Love, R. F. Love, J. D. Hart, John Frier, Will Duncan, L. L. Derrick, Charles Cochran, J. D. Black, Mack Fletcher, Bert Ancel, Robert Allie, W. P. Bird, Will Monteith, and John Catchings. Some

of these charter members are among the thirty-two cowboys comprising the primary study group for this volume.

Bibliography

Interviews and Letters

Adams, Glen to C. J. Brooks. Interviews. 1987–1989.

Beal, F. Logan to C. J. Brooks. Interview. January 17, 1990.

Benson, Lura to C. J. Brooks. Interview. January 17, 1990.

Binkley, Anemone Love to C. J. Brooks. Interview. January 3, 1990.

Breckon, Ira to C. J. Brooks. Interview. August, 17, 1990.

Dean, Graydon, Jr. to C. J. Brooks. Letter. December 13, 1989.

Dunlap, Pearl to C. J. Brooks. Interview. January 11, 1991.

Easley, Lorena to C. J. Brooks. Interview. December 20, 1990.

Fuchs, Cleo Heidel to C. J. Brooks. Interview. January 3, 1990.

Gray, Clifford to C. J. Brooks. Interview. January 16, 1990.

Howry, Lugene to C. J. Brooks. Interview. January 3, 1990.

Kizer, Faye McClure to C. J. Brooks. Interview. December 19, 1990.

Madera, Bert to C. J. Brooks. Interview. c. April 1988.

McGuffin, Margaret Walter to C. J. Brooks. Interview. January 3, 1990.

Medlin, Donna to C. J. Brooks. Interview. October 1988.

Shaw, Laverne Burk to C. J. Brooks. Interview. January 3, 1990.

Shelton, Sarah to C. J. Brooks. Interview. January 17, 1991.

Thorp, George to C. J. Brooks. Interview. January 3, 1990.

Thorp, Gladys to C. J. Brooks. Interview. January 17, 1990.

Tidwell, J. B. to C. J. Brooks. Interview. October 25, 1983.

Zimmerman, Bill to C. J. Brooks. Interview. April 25, 1990.

Collections

Lea County Cowboy Hall of Fame and Western Heritage Center Collection, New Mexico Junior College, Hobbs, New Mexico.

New Mexico Junior College Archival Collection, Pannell Library, Hobbs, New Mexico.

Government Documents

New Mexico Statistical Abstract. Albuquerque: University of New Mexico, 1989.

13th Census of the United States. 1910. New Mexico. Chaves County, Volume 2; Eddy County, Volume 4.

Newspapers

Galveston News, December 14, 1885.

Knowles News Plains Special, 1910.

Lovington Leader, June 1952.

Lovington Press, October 9, 1958.

Odessa American, November 2, 1958.

Theses and Dissertations

Fenton, James Irving. "Tom Ross: Outlaw and Stockman." Unpublished Masters Thesis, University of Texas at El Paso, 1979.

Rowan, James Elmer. "Agricultural Land Utilization in the Llano Estacado of Eastern New Mexico and Western Texas." Unpublished Doctoral Dissertation, University of Nebraska, 1960.

Books

Athearn, Robert G. *The Mythic West in Twentieth Century America.* Lawrence: University of Kansas Press, 1986.

Atherton, Lewis. *The Cattle Kings.* Bloomington: Indiana University Press, 1967.

Beal, F. Logan. "The Beal Family of Ranger Lake." In *Then and Now: Lea County Families.* Volume I, Lovington, New Mexico: Lea County Genealogical Society, 1979.

Bellah, Robert N., et al. *Habits of the Heart: Individualism and Commitment in American Life.* Berkeley: University of California Press, 1985.

Beverly, Bob. *Hobo of the Rangeland: 100 Laughs for 100 Cents,* n.p., n.d.

Billington, Ray Allen. *The Westward Movement in the United States.* Princeton, New Jersey: D. Van Nostrand Co., Inc., 1959.

Binkley, Anemone Love. *A Man Called Jim.* Privately printed, 1986.

Clemens, Gus. *Legacy: The Story of the Permian Basin Region of West Texas and Southeast New Mexico.* San Antonio: Mulberry Avenue Books, 1983.

Cook, James H. *Fifty Years on the Frontier: As Cowboy, Hunter, Guide, Scout, and Ranchman.* Norman: University of Oklahoma Press, 1963.

Cowhands of the XIT, Dalhart, Texas, 1939.

Dary, David. *Cowboy Culture: A Saga of Five Centuries.* New York: Avon, 1981.

Dawson, John C., Sr. *High Plains Yesterdays: From XIT Days Through Drouth and Depression.* Austin: Eakin Press, 1985.

Dobie, J. Frank. *A Vaquero of the Brush Country.* Dallas: The Southwest Press, 1929.

Duke, Cordelia Sloan and Joe B. Frantz, *6,000 Miles of Fence.* Austin: University of Texas Press, 1961.

Early Settlers of Terry: A History of Terry County, Texas. Hereford, Texas: Pioneer Book Publishers, Inc., 1968.

Etulain, Richard W. "Western Fiction and History." In *The American West: New Perspectives, New Dimensions,* Jerome O. Steffen, editor. Norman: University of Oklahoma Press, 1979.

Forbis, William H. *The Cowboys (The Old West Series)*. New York: Time, Inc., 1973.

Frantz, Joe B. and Julian Ernest Choate, Jr. *The American Cowboy: The Myth and the Reality.* Norman: University of Oklahoma Press, 1955.

The Gaines County Story: A History of Gaines County, Texas. Seagraves, Texas: Pioneer Book Publishers, 1974.

Haley, J. Evetts. *Charles Goodnight: Cowman and Plainsman.* Norman: University of Oklahoma Press, 1949.

———. *Men of Fiber.* El Paso: Carl Hertzog, 1963.

The Handy Book for Genealogists. Logan, Utah: The Everton Publishers, Inc., 1967.

Harris, Charles and Buck Rainey, editors. *The Cowboy: Six Shooters, Songs, and Sex.* Norman: University of Oklahoma Press, 1976.

Hartshorne, Thomas L. *The Distorted Image: Changing Conceptions of the American Character Since Turner.* Cleveland: The Press of Case Western Reserve University, 1968.

Hedgpeth, Don. *The Texas Breed: A Cowboy Anthology.* Flagstaff: Northland Press, 1978.

Hendrix, John. *If I Can Do It Horseback: A Cow-Country Sketchbook.* Austin: University of Texas Press, 1964.

Hinshaw, Gil. *Lea, New Mexico's Last Frontier.* Hobbs, New Mexico: Hobbs Daily News-Sun, 1976.

The Historical Encyclopedia of New Mexico. Albuquerque, New Mexico: New Mexico Historical Association, 1945.

Bibliography

Holden, William Curry. *Alkali Trails: Or Social and Economic Movements of the Texas Frontier 1846–1900.* Dallas: The Southwest Press, 1930.

Lewis, Alfred Henry. *Wolfville Nights,* 1902. Cited by William W. Savage, Jr., *Cowboy Life: Reconstructing an American Myth.* Norman: University of Oklahoma Press, 1975.

Manis, Michelle. *The Beasley Connection,* Volume I, n.p., 1984.

Marshall, James M. *Land Fever: Dispossession and Frontier Myth.* Lexington: University Press of Kentucky, 1986.

McCauley, Jim. *A Stove-up Cowboy's Story.* Cited by Don Hedgpeth, *The Texas Breed,* p. 37. Flagstaff: Northland Press, 1978.

Meinig, D. W. *Imperial Texas: An Interpretive Essay in Cultural Geography.* Austin: University of Texas Press, 1969.

Mosley, May Price. *"Little Texas" Beginnings in Southeastern New Mexico.* Roswell, New Mexico: Hall-Poorbaugh Press, 1973.

The National Atlas of the United States of America. Washington, D. C.: United States Department of the Interior, Geological Survey, 1970.

Oden, Bill. *Early Days on the Texas-New Mexico Plains.* Canyon, Texas: Palo Duro Press, 1965.

Parks, Rita. *The Western Hero in Film and Television: Mass Media Mythology.* Ann Arbor, Michigan: UMI Research Press, 1982.

Pierarski, Vicki. "Cowboys, Cattlemen, and the Cattle Industry." In *The Frontier Experience: A Reader's Guide to the Life and Literature of the American West.* Jon Tuska and Vicki Pierarski, editors. Jefferson, North Carolina: McFarland and Company, 1984.

Pioneer Atlas of the American West: Containing Facsimile Reproductions of Maps and Indexes from the 1876 First Edition. Chicago: Rand McNally & Company, 1956.

Price, Eugene H. *Open Range Ranching on the South Plains in the 1890s.* Clarendon, Texas: Clarendon Press, 1967.

Prose and Poetry of the Live Stock Industry of the United States. Cited by William W. Savage, Jr., *Cowboy Life: Reconstructing an American Myth.* Norman: University of Oklahoma Press, 1975.

Rice, Ruth Kessler. *Letters from New Mexico 1899–1904.* Albuquerque, New Mexico: Adobe Press, 1981.

Savage, William W., Jr. *The Cowboy Hero: His Image in American History and Culture.* Norman: University of Oklahoma Press, 1979.

————, editor. *Cowboy Life: Reconstructing an American Myth.* Norman: University of Oklahoma Press, 1975.

————. "The Cowboy Myth." In *The Cowboy: Six Shooters, Songs, and Sex.* Charles Harris and Buck Rainey, editors. Norman: University of Oklahoma Press, 1976.

Shinkle, James D. *Fifty Years of Roswell History, 1867–1917.* Roswell, New Mexico: Hall-Poorbaugh Press, 1964.

Simpson, S. R. *Llano Estacado: or the Plains of West Texas.* San Antonio: The Naylor Company, 1957.

Skaggs, Jimmy M. *The Cattle-Trailing Industry: Between Supply and Demand, 1866–1890.* Lawrence: The University Press of Kansas, 1973.

Steffen, Jerome O., editor. "Insular v. Cosmopolitan Frontiers: A Proposal for the Comparative Study of American Frontiers," *The American West: New Perspectives, New Dimensions.* Norman: University of Oklahoma Press, 1979.

————. *Comparative Frontiers: A Proposal for Studying the American West.* Norman: University of Oklahoma Press, 1980.

Then and Now: Lea County Families. Volume I. Lovington, New Mexico: Lea County Genealogical Society, 1979.

Then and Now: Lea County Families. Volume II. Lovington, New Mexico: Lea County Genealogical Society, 1984.

Tobin, Gregory M. *The Making of a History: Walter Prescott Webb and "The Great Plains."* Austin: University of Texas Press, 1976.

Tuska, Jon and Vicki Pierarski, editors. *The Frontier Experience: A Reader's Guide to the Life and Literature of the American West.* Jefferson, North Carolina: McFarland and Company, 1984.

Wallis, George A. *Cattle Kings of the Staked Plains.* Denver: Sage Books, 1964.

Weigle, Marta and Peter White. *The Lore of New Mexico.* Albuquerque: University of New Mexico Press, 1988.

Westermeier, Clifford P. "The Cowboy and Sex." In *The Cowboy: Six-Shooters, Songs, and Sex.* Charles Harris and Buck Rainey, editors. Norman: University of Oklahoma Press, 1976.

————. *Trailing the Cowboy: His Life and Lore as Told by Frontier Journalists.* Caldwell, Idaho: Caxton Printers, 1955.

Whitlock, V. H. *Cowboy Life on the Llano Estacado.* Norman: University of Oklahoma Press, 1970.

Wiggins, Walt. *New Mexico Cockleburs and Cow Chips.* Roswell, New Mexico: Western Heritage Press, 1975.

Periodicals

Ball, Eve. "Henry Record was Muy Hombre," *Frontier Times,* February–March 1976, pp. 62–64.

Beverly, Bob. "No Life for a Tenderfoot," *The Cattleman,* June 1950, p. 40.

———. "That Flaxey Horse," *The Cattleman,* November 1952, p. 100.

———. "The Old Y Crossing," *The Cattleman,* February 193, p. 125.

"The Cowboy's Life," *El anunciador de Trinidad,* December 1, 1887. Cited by Clifford P. Westermeier, *Trailing the Cowboy: His Life and Lore as Told by Frontier Journalists.* Caldwell, Idaho: Caxton Printers, 1955.

Davis, David Brion. "Ten Gallon Hero," *American Quarterly,* Summer 1954, pp. 112–14.

Gates, Paul William. "The Homestead Law in an Incongruous Land System," *American Historical Review,* July 1936, p. 656.

Mallory, J. Albert. "The Cowboy of Today," *Out West: A Magazine of the Old Pacific and the New,* January–June 1908, p. 224.

McMurtry, Larry. "Take My Saddle from the Wall," *Harpers,* September 1968, p. 45. Cited by Clifford P. Westermeier, "The Cowboy and Sex," in *The Cowboy: Six-Shooters, Songs, and Sex.* Norman: University of Oklahoma Press, 1976.

Pomeroy, Earl. "Toward a Reorientation of Western History: Continuity and Environment," *Mississippi Valley Historical Review,* June 1954–March 1955, pp. 581–82.

Bibliography

Shannon, Fred A. "The Homestead Act and the Labor Surplus," *American Historical Review,* July 1936.

Texas Live Stock Journal, January 21, 1888, p. 15. Cited by Clifford P. Westermeier, *Trailing the Cowboy: His Life and Lore as Told by Frontier Journalists.* Caldwell, Idaho: Caxton Printers, 1955.

Index

The Last Cowboys was designed by Harold Augustus
and composed on a AST Premium 386/25 computer,
using PageMaker 4.0 with 11/14 Century Old Style from the
Adobe Type Library.
Printed and bound by Thomson-Shore, Inc.,
on 50 lb. natural offset.